# THE BEST JOKE BOOK EVER!

## AURA

This edition printed in 2015 by Baker & Taylor (UK) Ltd, Bicester, Oxfordshire, OX26 4ST

Licensed exclusively to Top That Publishing Ltd

Tide Mill Way, Woodbridge, Suffolk, IP12 1AP, UK

www.topthatpublishing.com

Copyright © 2015 Tide Mill Media

0 2 4 6 8 9 7 5 3 1

Manufactured in China

Teacher: Did your big sister help you with your homework?

Pupil: No Miss, she did it all herself.

Mum: From now on you're going to have free school dinners.

Son: But Mum, I don't want three school dinners, one is more than enough.

Teacher: I'd like to go through one whole day without having to tell you off.

Pupil: You have my permission.

Pupil 1: Our teacher talks to herself. Does yours?

Pupil 2: Yes, but she doesn't realise it. She thinks we're actually listening!

**Pupil: Laugh and the class laughs with you.**

**Teacher: But you get detention alone.**

**Why is a teacher like an elephant?**

**Stick chalk up his nostrils and you'll find out.**

**Teacher: Why didn't you answer me?**

**Pupil: I did. I shook my head.**

**Teacher: You don't expect me to hear it rattling from here, do you?**

Teacher: Be sure that you go straight home.

Pupil: I can't, I live just round the corner!

Pupil: I didn't do my homework because I lost my memory.

Teacher: When did this start?

Pupil: When did what start?

Teacher: What makes your mother an expert on Ancient Greece?

Pupil: She never cleans the frying pan.

What do you call someone who carries on talking when nobody is listening?

A teacher.

Dad: When I was your age I thought nothing of walking five miles to school.

Son: I agree, I don't think much of it myself.

Teacher: What did the Israelites do after crossing the Red Sea?

Pupil: Dry themselves off.

Pupil: I don't like cheese with holes.

Dinner lady: Well just eat the cheese and leave the holes on the side of your plate.

How do school children know when the weekend is over?

It stops raining.

**Teacher:** Which English king was good at fractions?

**Pupil:** Henry the 1/8.

**Teacher:** Who was Joan of Arc's father?

**Pupil:** Noah, Miss.

**Teacher:** Who fought in World War II?

**Pupil:** My great grandfather, Sir.

**Teacher:** How do we know that Christopher Columbus was economical?

**Pupil:** Because he went thousands of miles on one galleon, Sir.

**Teacher:** Why do penguins never meet polar bears?

**Pupil:** Because they don't like each other.

**Teacher:** What lies at both ends of the Straits of Gibraltar?

**Pupil:** Er, the bends of Gibraltar?

**Teacher:** What is a plate boundary?

**Pupil:** It's where you put your knife and fork.

**Teacher:** Why are you the only one in today?

**Pupil:** Because I missed school dinner yesterday.

8

**Pupil:** This egg is bad.

**Dinner lady:** Don't blame me, I only laid the table.

**Dinner lady:** It's rude to reach over the table, haven't you got a tongue in your head?

**Pupil:** Yes, but my arms are longer.

**Pupil:** There's a dead fly in my dinner.

**Cook:** Oh dear, I wonder if it died after tasting it.

**Teacher:** What is the capital of Canada?

**Pupil:** C.

Teacher: Where are the Great Plains?

Pupil: At the great airports, Sir.

Dinner lady: Eat up your greens, they are good for your skin.

Pupil: But I don't want green skin.

What do pixies and elves do after school?

Their gnomework.

Son: Dad, can you help me find the lowest common denominator?

Father: Haven't they found it yet? They couldn't find it when I was at school!

Son: Dad, can you help me on homework about the Iron Age?

Father: Sorry son, I'm a bit rusty on that.

Sports teacher: What form are you in boy?

Pupil: Well, I scored two goals last Saturday, Sir.

Mother: Do you really think my daughter has a photographic memory?

Teacher: Yes, but nothing ever seems to develop.

Teacher: What is a forum?

Pupil: Two-um plus two-um.

Daughter: I got into trouble because I didn't know where the Pyramids were.

Father: It's time you learnt to remember where you left things.

What kind of mathematical powder would you find in the Maths room?

Talc-ulators.

Mother: What do you think Sammy will be when he's passed all his exams?

Father: A pensioner.

Mother: Did you have your school medical exam?

Daughter: Yes. I got one out of ten.

Teacher: What does BC stand for?

Pupil: Before Calculators.

Where do naughty ghosts have to stand at school?

In the horror-doors.

Teacher: Please don't talk while you're doing your exam.

Pupil: We're only talking – we're not doing the exam.

Which school subject are snakes best at?

Hiss-tory.

Teacher: Do you understand the importance of punctuation, Peter?

Peter: Yes Sir, I'm always on time.

How do schools of fish get home? By octo-bus.

Teacher: You're late Jenny, we start at nine o'clock.

Jenny: That's OK Miss, I don't mind you starting without me.

How does a witch get her lunch to school?

She packs it in her school hag.

What's the difference between school dinners and a pile of slugs?

School dinners come on a plate.

Teacher: Who can tell me what 'dogma' means?

Pupil: It's a lady dog that's had puppies, Sir.

What's the difference between a poisonous snake and a teacher?

The snake makes a good pet.

What's a wizard's favourite subject?

Spelling.

Did you hear about the naughty wizard at school?

He was ex-spelled.

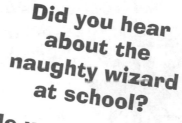

What do you call an ant that skips school?

A tru-ant.

Teacher: What did you get for Christmas, Tommy?

Tommy: A drum kit, Sir. It's the best present I ever got.

Teacher: Why's that?

Tommy: Because my mum gives me £1 a week not to play it.

**Teacher:** You can't bring that lamb to school – what about the smell?

**Mary:** It's ok, Miss – she'll get used to it.

**Teacher:** What is a polygon?

**Pupil:** A dead parrot, Sir.

**Headteacher:** Teachers like Mr Sneer don't grow on trees you know.

**Cheeky pupil:** No, they just swing in them.

**Teacher:** If I cut two apples into twenty pieces and three oranges into fifteen pieces, what do I have?

**Pupil:** A fruit salad.

How do bees get to school?

By school buzz.

Did you hear about the posh school where all the pupils smelled?

It was for filthy rich kids.

Teacher: What's the theory of relativity about?

Pupil: Aunts, uncles, cousins...

Teacher: Harry! You can't sleep in my class!

Harry: I could if you stopped talking, Sir.

Teacher: Who was the first man on the moon?

Pupil: A spaceman, Sir.

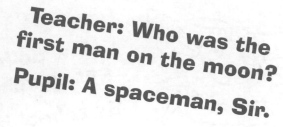

What do religious Maths teachers say?

"Go forth and multiply."

Teacher: Why did the Romans build straight roads?

Pupil: To stop their soldiers going round the bend.

Teacher: Which liquid can never freeze?

Pupil: Hot water, Miss.

Teacher: Sir, I don't think I deserved a zero in my Maths test.

Pupil: Neither do I, but there isn't a lower score.

Teacher: How do you find a square root?

Pupil: Look for a square vegetable, Miss.

Teacher: What do we use a Bunsen burner for?

Pupil: Burning bunsens, Sir.

What's the difference between school and chocolate?

People like chocolate.

Teacher: If you saw me standing by a witch, which fruit would it remind you of?

Pupil: A pear, Miss.

Why is the school swot like quicksand?

Because everything sinks into him.

Teacher: Can anyone tell me what a shamrock is?

Pupil: It's a fake diamond, Miss.

Did you hear about the boy who couldn't get to grips with decimals?

He couldn't see the point.

Why did the flea fail its exams?

Because it wasn't up to scratch.

Which is the longest piece of furniture at school?

The multiplication table.

Teacher: Have you any brothers or sisters?

Pupil: No, Sir. I'm an only child.

Teacher: Thank goodness for that.

What do you get if you cross old potatoes with lumpy gravy?

School dinners.

What's the difference between a schoolboy and an angler?

One baits his hooks and the other hates his books.

What should you remember in Chemistry?

Never lick the spoon.

Teacher: Can anyone tell me what geese eat?

Pupil: Gooseberries, Sir.

Teacher: Who can tell me where Hadrian's Wall is?

Pupil: I expect it's around Hadrian's garden Miss.

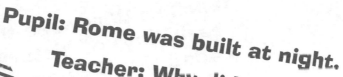

**Pupil:** Rome was built at night.

**Teacher:** Why did you say that?

**Pupil:** Because it wasn't built in a day.

**Teacher:** Which mineral do we import from America?

**Pupil:** Coca-Cola, Sir.

What did the bookworm say to the librarian?

"Can I burrow this book please?"

What are you going to be when you get out of school?

An old man.

**Teacher:** Why were the early days of history called the dark ages?

**Pupil:** Because there were so many knights.

What did Caesar say to Cleopatra?

Toga-ether we can rule the world.

**Teacher:** Who invented King Arthur's round table?

**Pupil:** Cir-cumference, Miss.

**Teacher:** Why did Arthur have a round table?

**Pupil:** So no one could corner him, Sir.

**Teacher: Where is the English Channel?**

**Pupil: I don't know – my TV doesn't pick it up.**

**What is the most popular sentence at school?**

**I don't know.**

**Teacher: Why does the Statue of Liberty stand in New York harbour?**

**Pupil: Because it can't sit down.**

**Teacher: You missed school yesterday didn't you?**

**Pupil: Not very much.**

Father: What did you learn in school today?

Son: Not enough, I have to go back tomorrow.

Mother: How was your first day?

Son: It was OK except for some man called 'Teacher' who kept spoiling our fun.

Daughter: I'm not going back to school ever again.

Father: Why not?

Daughter: The teacher's stupid. All she does is ask questions.

Teacher: What can you tell me about the Dead Sea?

Pupil: Dead? I didn't even know it was sick!

Teacher: What is a circle?

Pupil: It's a round straight line with a hole in it.

Teacher: Are you having trouble hearing?

Pupil: No, I'm having trouble listening.

Teacher: Why were you late?

Pupil: Sorry, Sir. I overslept.

Teacher: You mean you need to sleep at home too?

Some people say the school dinners are out of this world.

Most pupils wish they were out of their stomachs.

**Teacher:** Can you tell me something that conducts electricity?

**Pupil:** Why, er...

Which trees do you find in a classroom?

Beech-ers.

**Mother:** What was the first thing you learned in class?

**Daughter:** How to talk without moving my lips.

**Teacher:** How can you make so many mistakes in one day?

**Pupil:** I get up early!

Teacher: Class, we will only have half a day this morning.

Class: Hooray!

Teacher: We will have the rest after lunch.

Teacher: Are you good at arithmetic?

Paul: Well, yes and no.

Teacher: What do you mean?

Paul: Yes, I'm no good at arithmetic.

Old man: When I was at school I was as smart as the next fellow.

Old woman: It's a pity the next fellow was an idiot.

When is a blue school book not a blue school book?

When it is read.

Why is the classroom like a car?

Because it's full of nuts and has a crank at the front.

Why is a pencil the heaviest thing in your bag?

Because it's full of lead.

Art teacher: Which colours would you paint the sun and the wind?

Pupil: The sun rose and the wind blue.

Teacher: What sort of birds do we get in captivity?

Pupil: Jailbirds, Miss.

Teacher: Did you see the Catskill Mountains on your visit to America?

Pupil: No, but I saw them kill mice.

What's black and white and horrible?

A Maths exam paper.

Teacher: What are the small rivers that run into the Nile?

Pupil: The juve-niles, Sir.

Dinner lady: Eat your roast beef, it's full of iron.

Pupil: No wonder it's so tough.

What did the children do when there were rock cakes for lunch?

They took their pick.

School inspector (to pupil): How many teachers work in this school?

Pupil: About half of them, Sir.

Why is school like a shower?

One wrong turn and you're in hot water.

Teacher: Recite your tables, please.

Pupil: Kitchen table, dining table, bedside table...

Did you hear about the school near the chicken farm?

The pupils picked up fowl language.

Teacher: What is the longest night of the year?

Pupil: A fortnight.

Teacher: Your homework looks as if it is in your father's handwriting!

Pupil: Well, I used his pen, Sir.

Pupil: My lunch has got hairs in it.

Dinner lady: Well, it is rabbit pie!

Did you hear about the boy who spent hours on his homework each night?

He kept it under his mattress.

Teacher: Why do birds fly south for winter?

Pupil: Because it's too far to walk.

Mother: Did you get a good place in the exam?

Daughter: Sure, I sat next to the brainiest kid in the class.

Why did the teacher put the lights on?

Because the class was so dim.

Pupil: I've just swallowed a bone.

Dinner lady: Are you choking?

Pupil: No, I'm serious.

Teacher: Tommy, put some more water in the fish tank please.

Pupil: He hasn't drunk yesterday's yet!

PE Teacher: Why didn't you stop the ball?

Pupil (in goal): I thought that's what the net was for!

Teacher: What's the best way to pass this geometry test?

Pupil: Knowing all the angles, Miss.

Schoolboy to his friend: My dad is so old, when he was at school, history was called current affairs!

Which capital city cheats at exams?

Peking.

Teacher: In this exam you will be allowed ten minutes for each question.

Pupil: How long is the answer?

What would you get if you crossed a vampire and a teacher?

Lots of blood tests.

Teacher: I hope I didn't see you looking at Fred's test paper.

Pupil: I hope you didn't see me either.

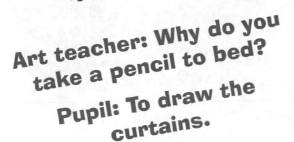

Art teacher: Why do you take a pencil to bed?

Pupil: To draw the curtains.

What kinds of tests do they give witches?

Hex-aminations.

Teacher: Were you copying his sums?

Pupil: No Sir. I'm just seeing if he got mine right.

Teacher: Can anyone tell me what sort of animal a slug is?

Pupil: It's a snail with a housing problem.

Father: What did you learn at school today?

Son: I learnt that those sums you did for me were wrong.

Teacher: Simon, can you spell your name backwards?

Simon: No Miss.

Teacher: What happens to gold when it is exposed to the air?

Pupil: It gets stolen.

Teacher: Why do some animals have fur coats?

Pupil: Because they would look silly in plastic macs, Sir.

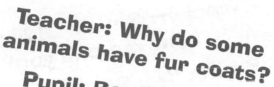

Teacher: Make up a sentence using the word lettuce.

Pupil: Let us out of school early!

Teacher: Why are you so late?

Pupil: I was obeying the sign that says, "School ahead. Go slow!"

Teacher: When do you like school most?

Pupil: When it's closed.

**Teacher:** Smith! Didn't you hear me call you?

**Smith:** Yes, Sir, but you told us not to answer back.

**Teacher:** Why can't your nose be twelve inches long?

**Pupil:** It would be a foot!

**Teacher:** Give me a sentence with the words defence, defeat and detail in it.

**Pupil:** When a horse jumps over defence, defeat go before detail.

Why is 6 afraid of 7?

Because 7, 8, 9.

**Teacher:** If you had five apples on your desk and the boy next to you took three what would you have?

**Pupil:** A fight.

**Teacher:** Do you want to borrow a pocket calculator?

**Pupil:** No thanks. I know how many pockets I have.

**Teacher:** What is a comet?

**Pupil:** A star with a tail.

**Teacher:** Can you name one?

**Pupil:** Lassie.

Do you ever get straight As?

No, but I sometimes get crooked Bs.

**Teacher:** Can you tell me how to use the word 'politics'?

**Pupil:** My parrot swallowed a watch and now Polly ticks.

Why do camels make good teachers?

Because they've always got the hump.

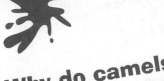

**Teacher:** Tommy, you try my patience.

**Tommy:** No, Miss, you had better try mine. There's more of it.

**Father:** Are you in the top half of your class?

**Daughter:** No, I'm one of the students who make the top half possible.

**Teacher:** Would you at the back of the room stop passing notes.

**Pupil:** We're not passing notes. We're playing cards.

**Teacher:** Do you file your nails Janine?

**Janine:** No, I just throw them away.

**Art teacher:** The picture of the horse is good, but where is the wagon?

**Pupil:** The horse will draw it.

**Teacher:** Which birds are found in Portugal?

**Pupil:** Portu-geese.

Mother: How did you find school today?

Daughter: I just got off the bus and there it was.

Teacher: Why are you picking your nose in class?

Pupil: My mother won't let me do it at home.

Teacher: Why are you reading the last pages of your history book first?

Pupil: I want to know how it ends.

Teacher: Name three famous poles?

Pupil: North, south and tad.

Teacher: What do we do with crude oil?

Pupil: Teach it some manners.

Teacher: Give me three reasons why the world is round.

Pupil: My dad, my mum and you all say so.

Teacher: Jimmy, stop your day dreaming!

Jimmy: I wasn't day dreaming, I was taking a nap.

Teacher: How do you know carrots are good for your eyes?

Pupil: I've never seen a rabbit wearing glasses.

What's the difference between school tapioca and frog spawn?

Not a lot!

Who is the patron saint of school playgrounds?

St Francis of a see-saw.

Teacher: Have any of you read the Bible?

Class: No, Miss – we're waiting for the film.

What's yellow and writes essays?

A ballpoint banana.

Pupil: Our school is always on fire.

Friend: Why is that?

Pupil: Because all the kids wear blazers.

Why did the books get out of the school bag?

Because they were exercise books.

Did you hear about the school bully who dangled a kid from the roof?

He got suspended.

Mother: How do you know Jimmy plays truant?

Teacher: Jimmy? Who's Jimmy?

What's the difference between a teacher and a train?

The train goes "chew - chew". The teacher says, "Spit that gum out!"

Where do aliens go to study?

Mooniversity.

Father: So you say that Susie's brains are in her boots.

Teacher: I'm afraid so – and she comes to school in her trainers.

Why was the astronomer told off at school?

She kept staring into space.

What did it say on the alien's school report?

"This pupil's work is out of this world."

Teacher: How long can someone live without a brain?

Pupil: How old are you, Sir?

Mother: Did you enjoy your first day at school?

Daughter: First day? You mean I have to go back again?

Where are teachers made?

On an assembly line.

**Mother:** Why have you sent Jimmy to his room?

**Father:** He gets his report tomorrow and I'm out tomorrow night.

**Teacher:** Who were the first people to write using fountain pens?

**Pupil:** The Incas, Miss.

**Teacher:** How fast does light travel?

**Pupil:** Too fast – it always comes too early in the morning.

**Teacher:** I wish you would pay a little attention!

**Pupil:** I'm paying as little as I can.

**Teacher:** Why did you put that frog in Michelle's desk?

**Boy:** Because I couldn't find a mouse.

**Teacher:** You should have been here at nine.

**Pupil:** Why? What happened?

**Teacher:** Your spelling is terrible.

**Pupil:** What do you mean? That's my algebra.

**Mother:** Do you know a girl called Penny Richards?

**Daughter:** Yes, she sleeps next to me in Maths.

**Teacher:** Your essay about your cat is the same as your sister's.

**Pupil:** Yes, it's the same cat.

Our school canteen must be spotlessly clean – all the food tastes of soap.

**Teacher:** Describe water for me.

**Pupil:** It's a colourless liquid that goes black when I put my hands in it.

Sign on school notice board:

The school concert starts at eight sharp and ends at ten flat.

**What kind of ships do students travel on?**

**Scholarships.**

**Why was the teacher fired?**

**He didn't have enough class.**

**What did the anatomy teacher say at the beginning of his lesson?**

**Is every body here?**

**Teacher: Which language do they speak in Cuba?**

**Pupil: Cubic.**

**Teacher: What's the Equator?**

**Pupil: It's an imaginary lion running around the Earth.**

**Why is history the sweetest lesson?**

**Because it's full of dates.**

**Teacher: Give me a sentence with the word 'centimetre' in it.**

**Pupil: My grandma arrived at the station and I was centimetre.**

**Why did the teacher yell at Humpty Dumpty?**

**Because he cracked up in class.**

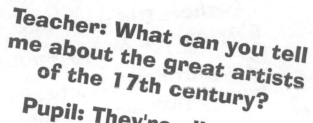

**Teacher:** What can you tell me about the great artists of the 17th century?

**Pupil:** They're all dead.

**Teacher:** What did the Gauls use to write on?

**Pupil:** Gall stones, Miss.

**Teacher:** Why did Henry VIII have so many wives?

**Pupil:** Because he liked to chop and change.

**Teacher:** I want you to write an essay on Attila the Hun.

**Pupil:** I'd rather write it on paper.

Father: Did your school play have a happy ending?

Daughter: Well, everyone was happy when it ended.

Why do children go to school?

Because school won't go to them.

Mother: How are you getting on at school?

Son: Well, I'm centre forward in football and right back in lessons.

Why did the cyclops close his school?

Because he only had one pupil.

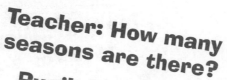

Teacher: How many
seasons are there?

Pupil: Two, Sir –
football and cricket.

Teacher: Who was
the Black Prince?

Pupil: The son of Old
King Coal.

Father: Why did you fail
your history exam?

Son: Because all the
questions were about
things that happened
before I was born.

Teacher:
In history, what was half
animal and half man?

Pupil: Buffalo Bill.

Teacher: Why are you late for school?

Pupil: There are eight people in our family and the alarm clock was set for seven.

What has a teacher got that his pupils haven't?

The answer book.

Teacher: If we breathe oxygen in the daytime, what do we breathe at night?

Pupil: Nitrogen.

Teacher: Where was the Declaration of Independence signed?

Pupil: At the bottom.

Teacher: If this class doesn't stop making so much noise I'll go crazy!

Class: Too late, we haven't made a sound for an hour!

Teacher: Why was Shakespeare able to write so well?

Pupil: Because where there's a Will there's a way.

Teacher: Where would you find the Andes?

Pupil: At the end of the wristies.

Teacher: Which pine has the sharpest needles?

Pupil: Porcupine.

**Teacher:** Name something with a big horn that's very dangerous.

**Pupil:** A motor car.

**Teacher:** What is hail?

**Pupil:** Hard-boiled rain.

**Headmaster (to visitor):** What was the first thing that struck you in the school chemistry lab?

**Visitor:** A paper plane.

**Teacher:** Do you know the population of London?

**Pupil:** No, I've never been there.

**Teacher:** Can you name the four seasons?

**Pupil:** Salt, pepper, mustard and vinegar.

**Teacher:** What is an asset?

**Pupil:** A young donkey?

**Teacher:** What do we call a person who is very talkative but uninteresting?

**Pupil:** A teacher.

**Teacher:** Whose emblem is the leek?

**Pupil:** The plumbers'.

Teacher: Why does the Earth turn around the Sun?

Pupil: Because it doesn't want to get toasted on just one side.

Why was the cannibal expelled from school?

He kept buttering up the teacher.

Teacher: How many days of the week begin with the letter t?

Pupil: Four. Tuesday, Thursday, today and tomorrow.

Pupil: Sir, everyone's ignoring me!

Teacher: Who said that?

Teacher: If you had twelve sweets, and Johnny took half, what would he have?

Pupil: A black eye.

Pupil: I can't read this correction Sir.

Teacher: It says you must write more clearly.

Teacher: Tommy, what is one fifth of three seventeenths?

Tommy: I don't know, but it isn't enough to worry about.

Music teacher: Why have you written "blow, suck, blow, suck, blow, suck"?

Pupil: It's the music for my mouth organ.

Why didn't the gnome go to school yesterday?

His mum kept him at home for elf reasons.

Teacher: What is an octagon?

Pupil: A dead octopus.

Teacher: What's the difference between a buffalo and a bison?

Pupil: You can wash your hands in a bison.

Teacher: What is lukewarm water?

Pupil: Water that looks warm but isn't.

Pupil: Please Miss, I swallowed a whistle in PE.

Teacher: Rubbish! Sit down and don't let me hear another peep out of you.

Pupil: Will our sausages be long?

Dinner lady: I don't know, we never measure them.

Teacher: If I have six potatoes and eight people to feed, how should I divide them up?

Pupil: Mash them.

Teacher: What came after the dinosaurs?

Pupil: Their tails.

Teacher: I don't like all this graffiti on the school walls.

Pupil: Well, tell me the bits you do like and I'll rub out the rest.

Pupil: Someone's built a wall in the playground.

Teacher: I know – I can't get over it.

Why did the teacher put a cake on her head?

She wanted to have her hair in a bun.

Pupil: Sir, my friend's got measles and I think I've got it, too.

Teacher: I've told you before about copying.

Teacher: Your nose has been running all morning!

Pupil: I know – I can't get it to walk.

What wears a white coat and melts in the sun?

A lollipop lady.

Pupil: Sorry I'm late, a dog was chasing me on my bike!

Teacher: I've told you not to lend your bike to dogs.

Music teacher: Why did Tchaikovsky write this piece in four flats?

Pupil: Because he had to keep moving house.

Excuses for being late...

"My mum thought it was Sunday and forgot to wake me up."

"Someone had glued the cereal packet closed and my mum wouldn't let me go to school without breakfast."

"I squeezed the toothpaste too hard and had to put it back in the tube."

Why is the school football pitch so soggy?

Because of all the dribbling.

Teacher: Why have you got a sausage roll behind your ear?

Dinner lady: I must have eaten my pencil!

Pupil 1: I don't think the Woodwork teacher likes me.

Pupil 2: He's teaching me to make a coffin.

Pupil: There's a nasty film on top of my soup!

Dinner lady: What do you expect? Star Wars?

Teacher: Why has the dinner lady got a fish behind her ear?

Pupil: It's her herring aid.

Teacher: You musn't fight – you should learn to give and take.

Pupil: I did – he took my ball and I gave him a black eye.

Pupil: Can I have a chicken leg?

Dinner lady: Haven't you got a leg of your own?

Pupil: I is...

Teacher: No, it's 'I am'.

Pupil: OK. I am the ninth letter of the alphabet.

Pupil: Can I have two apples today?

Dinner lady: You must think they grow on trees!

**Woodwork teacher: How did you find using the drill?**

**Pupil: Very boring.**

**Teacher: I've spent hours giving you extra homework and you still can't add.**

**Pupil: I can add insult to injury.**

**Dentist: Why are you crying? It's all over.**

**Boy: I know, I have to go back to school now.**

**Teacher: Can you tell me what goldfish are?**

**Pupil: Rich sardines, Sir.**

Teacher: What is wasted energy?

Pupil: Telling a bald man a hair-raising story.

Caretaker: I'd like to join the football team.

PE teacher: Why?

Caretaker: I'd make a good sweeper.

What's worse than being kept in detention?

The teacher turning up at your house before school.

PE teacher: Can you sprint fast?

Pupil: Yes, Sir. I ran half a mile yesterday and I caught up with my shadow.

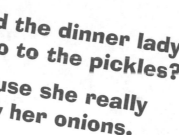

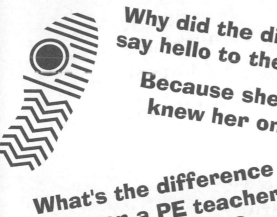

Why did the dinner lady say hello to the pickles?

Because she really knew her onions.

What's the difference between a PE teacher and an athlete?

About thirty-five miles per hour.

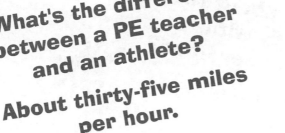

Teacher: When is the best time to gather fruit?

Pupil: When the farmer's dog is tied up.

Teacher: If six eggs cost sixty pence, how many would you get for twenty pence?

Pupil: None – I don't like eggs.

Teacher: Name something raised in a damp climate.

Pupil: An umbrella, Sir.

Did you hear about the dinner lady with blancmange on her head?

She was in the pink.

Teacher: Where did King William die?

Pupil: On page 21, Sir.

Teacher: Correct this sentence: "Our teacher am in sight."

Pupil: Our teacher am a sight.

**Pupil: How can I improve my violin playing?**

**Music teacher: Leave it inside the case.**

**Pupil: Oh no! Mum's given me a hedgehog sandwich for lunch!**

**Teacher: I find that very hard to swallow.**

**How does Quasimodo bring his sandwiches to school?**

**In the Lunchpack of Notre-Dame.**

**Son: My teacher is really mean.**

**Mother: Why is that?**

**Son: He borrows my pencil to give me bad marks.**

Teacher: What is an exit?

Pupil: An entrance you go out of.

Teacher: Have your daughter's eyes been checked?

Mother: No, they've always been brown.

Teacher: Which animal is the highest form of life?

Pupil: A giraffe.

Teacher: I'd like to discuss Tommy's marks.

Tommy's mum: They're not marks, they're spots.

Father: Does Sally ever come first in anything?

Teacher: She's always first in the lunch queue.

How can you tell when the school bell isn't working?

The teacher is in the playground wringing his hands.

Teacher: In which battle was General Wolf killed?

Pupil: His last one, Sir.

Teacher: Why are you late today?

Pupil: I'm not – I'm early for tomorrow.

What do you get when you cross literature with school dinners?

War and Pizza.

Pupil: Sorry I'm late – it's my new Velcro pyjamas.

Teacher: How would that make you late?

Pupil: I couldn't tear myself out of bed.

What do you get when you cross Chemistry with French lessons?

Napoleon Blown-apart.

Teacher: What is an organiser?

Pupil: The man that plays music in church.

What do you get when you cross French lessons and school dinners?

The Trifle Tower.

Teacher: Give me a sentence with the word diploma in it.

Pupil: Our pipe burst so my dad called diploma.

What do you get when you cross Art lessons with a dog?

Ruff sketches.

Teacher: Is Benny any good at the high jump?

Pupil: No, Sir. He can hardly clear his throat.

**Art teacher: Have you any camel hair brushes?**

**Shop keeper: Sorry, there aren't many camels around here.**

**What do you get when you cross Biology lessons with the teachers?**

**A skeleton staff.**

**Teacher: What is air?**

**Pupil: A balloon with no skin.**

**What do you get when you cross History lessons and assembly?**

**It doesn't matter – it was over ages ago.**

**Teacher:** Put what's in your mouth in the bin!

**Pupil:** I can't, Sir – it's a mouth ulcer.

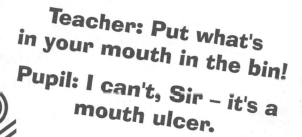

**Teacher:** Where's your essay on time travel?

**Pupil:** I haven't done it yet, but I'll hand it in last week.

**Teacher:** A fool can ask questions that wise people cannot answer.

**Pupil:** So that's why we failed our exams.

Did you hear what happened when the Chemistry teacher turned himself into a monster?

It was a big improvement.

Why did the dinner lady put bananas on her feet?

She wanted a pair of slippers.

Teacher: Why do you find the letter 'G' scary?

Pupil: Because it turns 'host' into 'ghost.'

Why did the dinner lady lock herself in the fridge?

She just wanted to chill.

Teacher: Today, we are going to charge a battery.

Pupil: Why? Doesn't it come to school for free like the rest of us?

Teacher: I don't want any of you blowing up the science lab.

Pupil: I don't think we could get our mouths round it.

Music teacher: Can you play the piano by ear?

Pupil: No, but my Dad fiddles with his whiskers.

Teacher: Why are your hands so dirty?

Pupil: Sorry, Sir – I thought it was Saturday.

Teacher: Where's your essay on Ancient Egypt?

Pupil: I didn't do it – but I've got a note from my mummy.

Teacher: How did you get that black eye?

Pupil: I sprained it doing my homework.

Teacher: I told you to write an essay on the Doomsday book.

Pupil: I couldn't get the book out of the museum.

Teacher: What do you think history lessons would have been like 200 years ago?

Pupil: Shorter.

Teacher: Can anyone define 'nothing'?

Pupil: Yes, Sir – it's the mark you gave me yesterday.

Teacher: Can you give me a long sentence?

Pupil: No, but I'd like to!

Teacher: Would you like to learn the dead languages?

Pupil: Oh yes, Sir – I want to be an undertaker.

Teacher: Your son spells atrociously.

Pupil's dad: Great! I can hardly spell that myself.

Teacher: Aren't you sorry you hit a smaller boy?

Pupil: Not as sorry as I would be if I'd hit a bigger one!

**What would happen if you took the school bus home?**

**The police would make you bring it back.**

**Guest at assembly: Well children, what shall I talk to you about?**

**Pupil: About five minutes!**

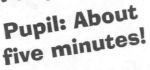

**Teacher: Name three kinds of nuts.**

**Pupil: Monkey nuts, chestnuts and forget-me-nuts.**

**What do you get when you cross Geography lessons with Sports Day?**

**Globetrotters.**

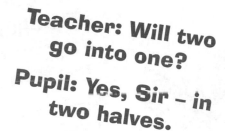

Teacher: Will two go into one?

Pupil: Yes, Sir – in two halves.

Teacher: You've missed a lot of history. How long have you been absent?

Pupil: Since the French Revolution.

Teacher: What is a mountain?

Pupil: A big lump of rock that slopes upwards.

Pupil: Our lollipop lady is really strong.

Teacher: Why do you say that?

Pupil: Because she holds up cars and buses.

**Teacher: Can anyone tell me where Ben Nevis is?**

**Pupil: He's not in this class, Sir.**

**Teacher: Who wrote Oliver Twist?**

**Pupil: How the Dickens should I know?**

**What do you get when you cross Art lessons with Maths lessons?**

**Painting by numbers.**

**Teacher: Why was the Forth bridge built?**

**Pupil: Because the other three fell down.**

What do you get when you cross English lessons with Music lessons?

Shakespeare, rattle and roll.

Teacher: Where's your essay on gravity?

Pupil: Sorry, Miss – I dropped it.

Teacher: What is a cannibal?

Pupil: A ball shot out of a cannon.

Teacher: Where's your essay on the digestive system?

Pupil: Sorry, Sir – the dog ate it.

Teacher: What is a Norseman?

Pupil: A man who rides an 'orse.

Teacher: Which countries are on the other side of the Atlantic?

Pupil: It depends which side you are on, Sir.

Teacher: Why does a zebra have stripes?

Pupil: If it didn't, it would be a horse.

What do you get when you cross a teacher with a tiger?

I don't know, but you'd better behave in its class!

Teacher: What is chivalry?

Pupil: It's when you feel cold all over.

Teacher: What is space?

Pupil: It's what's between your ears, Sir.

Teacher: Give me a sentence with the word 'analyse' in it.

Pupil: My sister Anna lies in bed until ten o'clock.

Teacher: What was Camelot famous for?

Pupil: Its knight life.

**Teacher: Which animals eat less than others?**

**Pupil: Moths – they eat holes in things.**

**What do you get when you cross Carpentry lessons with Drama?**

**Wooden acting.**

**Teacher: Name some stars.**

**Pupil: Football or film stars, Sir.**

**Why do kangaroos make good school inspectors?**

**Because they can catch teachers on the hop.**

Teacher: What do we get from India?

Pupil: India-gestion.

Father: Have you kept your position in class?

Son: Certainly – I started at the bottom and I'm still there.

Teacher: How many letters in 'blackbird'?

Pupil: Four.

Teacher: Eh? Spell it.

Pupil: c-r-o-w.

Did you hear about the python that was in love?

She had a crush on her teacher.

Why couldn't the leopard go to school?

Because it was covered in spots.

Pupil: Miss, Melissa keeps copying my work!

Teacher: Melissa! Come away from that photocopier.

Teacher: Have you ever seen an alien before, boy?

Pupil: No, Sir – you're the first.

Why wouldn't the oyster share its packed lunch?

It was a little shellfish.

**Teacher:** What is silence?

**Pupil:** Something you can't hear when you listen.

**Teacher:** Give me a sentence with the word 'miniature' in it?

**Pupil:** The miniature asleep you begin snoring.

**Teacher:** Who first built tunnels?

**Pupil:** Worms.

**Teacher:** I have an impression in my head. Can you tell me what an impression is?

**Pupil:** It's a dent in a soft place.

What type of school do gorillas go to?

A Kong-prehensive school.

Why didn't the snail go to school?

It did, but when it got there, it was time to go home again.

Teacher: Can you tell me something we buy by the metre?

Pupil: Gas, Sir.

Teacher: Aren't you fed up with being at the bottom of the class?

Pupil: No – it's warmer nearer the radiator.

Pupil: Sorry I'm late – I slipped and sprained my ankle.

Teacher: Another lame excuse.

Teacher: Late again! Does that school bus ever run on time?

Pupil: No, it runs on diesel.

Teacher: Putting a pin on a teacher's chair is an old joke.

Pupil: Ah, but it hasn't lost its point yet.

Pupil 1: We call our teacher 'Cocoa'.

Pupil 2: Why's that?

Pupil 1: Because she puts us to sleep.

Teacher: Did you give Jimmy a black eye?

Pupil: No. He already had the eye – I just blackened it.

Pupil 1: We call our teacher 'Balloon'.

Pupil 2: Why's that?

Pupil 1: Because he's full of hot air.

Teacher: Name a popular bank.

Pupil: Bank holiday?

Teacher: Why did the boy stand on the burning deck?

Pupil: Because it was too hot to sit down.

**Teacher:** Name something made from horn.

**Pupil:** Hornaments.

**Teacher:** What are you going to give your little brother for Christmas?

**Pupil:** I don't know. I gave him measles last year.

**Teacher:** Give me a sentence with the word 'gruesome' in it.

**Pupil:** My dad gruesome potatoes in his allotment.

**Teacher:** Give me a sentence with the word 'pasture' in it.

**Pupil:** I pasture house on the way to school.

Teacher: What comes before seven?

Pupil: The milkman, Sir.

Teacher: Why have you brought a hammer to school?

Pupil: Because we break up for the holidays today.

What do vampires always bring to school?

An apple for the creature.

Pupil 1: We call our teacher 'Treasure'.

Pupil 2: Why's that?

Pupil 1: Because we wonder where they dug him up.

**Father: Your teacher tells me it's impossible to teach you anything.**

**Son: I told you he was no good.**

**Teacher: Look at the map and tell me which is the warmer side of Scotland.**

**Pupil: The east – it's nearer the radiator.**

**Teacher: Which English king introduced wine to the country?**

**Pupil: Alfred the Grape.**

**Teacher: Correct this sentence: 'The toast was drank.'**

**Pupil: The toast was eaten.**

Teacher: Can you give me a proverb?

Pupil: A sock on the foot is worth two on the nose.

Pupil 1: We call our teacher 'Snowman'.

Pupil 2: Why's that?

Pupil 1: Because he's abominable.

Teacher: If I drop this pound coin into this chemical, will it dissolve?

Pupil: Doubt it, Sir – you're a skinflint.

Teacher: Why are you shouting and screaming?

Pupil: Because you are standing on my foot.

Teacher: Give me an example of a collective noun.

Pupil: A vacuum cleaner.

Teacher: Correct this sentence: 'It am very cold.'

Pupil: It am very hot.

Teacher 1: How was your lesson on electricity?

Teacher 2: Shocking.

Teacher: A biped is anything that goes on two feet. Can you give me an example?

Pupil: A pair of socks.

**Father: My son wants to be a racing driver – what should I do?**

**Teacher: Don't stand in his way.**

**Pupil: Miss! That boy is rolling his eyes at me.**

**Teacher: Pick them up and roll them back.**

**Why did the teacher wear a mortar board?**

**Because he was thick as a brick.**

**Teacher: I was angry yesterday when I heard a boy snoring in my lesson.**

**Pupil: So was I – it woke me up.**

**Teacher:** Can you read French?

**Pupil:** Yes, If it's written in English.

**Teacher:** If I said a man was creating a stir, what would he be doing?

**Pupil:** Making porridge.

**Teacher:** Don't bother me – I've a lot on my hands.

**Pupil:** Why not try soap and water?

**Teacher:** Is that your exam paper? The name is illegible.

**Pupil:** Can't be mine then – my name's Smith.

**Teacher:** What is a clean sweep?

**Pupil:** One that's had a bath.

**Teacher:** Why do you have a flower sticking out of your pocket?

**Pupil:** Because I'm a budding genius.

**Teacher:** The school orchestra played Mozart last night.

**Pupil:** Who won?

**Teacher:** Why are you always late for school?

**Pupil:** Because you always ring the bell before I get here.

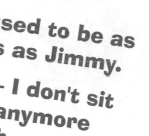

**Teacher:** You used to be as good at Maths as Jimmy.

**Pupil:** I know – I don't sit next to him anymore though.

**Pupil:** Can I be excused?

**French teacher:** Oui, oui.

**Pupil:** No, I just want to wash my hands.

**Teacher:** Why do swans have long necks?

**Pupil:** So that they don't drown at high tide.

**Teacher:** Where are your tonsils?

**Pupil:** I don't know, they were taken out years ago.

**Teacher: I hear the fencing team lost last night.**

**Pupil: Yes, foiled again.**

**Pupil 1: I wish Napoleon was Russian.**

**Pupil 2: Why?**

**Pupil 1: Because that's what I wrote in my exam.**

**Dinner lady 1: Why have you put that cake in the freezer?**

**Dinner lady 2: You said it needed icing.**

**What's the difference between Cinderella and the school goalkeeper?**

**Cinderella gets to the ball.**

Teacher: Where was King David's Temple?

Pupil: On King David's head.

Teacher: I thought I told you to write an essay on cheese.

Pupil: Have you tried writing on a piece of cheddar?

What's the difference between prison and school?

In prison you get off for good behaviour.

What did the policewoman's son say when he got home from school?

It's meema, meema, meema.

Teacher: I want you to write out 'I must not be late for school' one hundred times.

Pupil: But I was only late once.

Teacher: How dare you burp in front of me.

Pupil: Sorry, did you want to burp first?

Teacher: Where does sugar come from?

Pupil: From the lady next door.

Teacher: What do you think Julius Caesar would be doing if he were alive today?

Pupil: Drawing his pension.

Teacher: What is the plural of hippopotamus?
Pupil: Who'd want more than one?

Teacher: This note from your parents is completely blank.

Pupil: My parents were speechless when they saw my report.

Teacher: Why are you wrapped up so warmly?

Caretaker: I'm painting the school gates and it said to use two coats.

Teacher: Are you making fun of my hair?

Pupil: No, your hairdresser has done that already.

**Teacher:** What use is only being able to count to ten?

**Pupil:** I want to be a boxing referee.

**Pupil:** Why is there suntan lotion on these bananas?

**Dinner lady:** To stop them peeling.

**Dinner lady 1:** How do I make an apple crumble?

**Dinner lady 2:** Hit it with a hammer.

**Teacher:** In Britain, where are Kings and Queens crowned?

**Pupil:** On the head.

Teacher: What happened to sailors who didn't eat vegetables?

Pupil: They didn't get any pudding.

Teacher: Why were you whistling in class?

Pupil: I don't know the words.

Teacher: What is concrete made of?

Pupil: That's a hard question.

Teacher: Spell 'weather'.

Pupil: W-e-v-v-e-r.

Teacher: That's the worst spell of weather we've had for some time.

Teacher: What is a snail?

Pupil: A slug with a crash helmet.

Teacher: I've told you before about talking at the same time as I'm speaking.

Pupil: Well, you never stop talking.

Teacher: Order, children, order!

Pupil: Burger and chips please.

Teacher: Can you tell me what happened in 1066?

Pupil: I can't even remember what happened yesterday.

Teacher: What is memory?

Pupil: The thing you forget with.

Teacher: Why can't you answer any of my questions?

Pupil: What would be the use of coming here if I could?

Teacher: What is the capital of Iceland?

Pupil: 'I', Sir.

Teacher: Name three animals that live in the jungle.

Pupil: Two lions and a tiger.

**Teacher:** Why are you sitting in my desk?

**Pupil:** It's the first day of term – you said we could sit where we like.

**Teacher:** How many ribs have you got?

**Pupil:** I don't know – I'm too ticklish to count them.

**Teacher:** What is a yokel?

**Pupil:** The centre of an eggle.

**Teacher:** Did you have trouble with your French in Paris?

**Pupil:** No, but the Parisians did.

Mother: Do you like going to school?

Daughter: Oh yes – it's the staying there I don't like.

Teacher: Why do gardeners put dung on their strawberries?

Pupil: I dunno – I put cream on mine.

Teacher: To do anything in life, you need to start at the bottom and work up.

Pupil: What about swimming?

Teacher: What is a distant relative?

Pupil: My brother John – he lives in Australia.

**Teacher:** Any questions?

**Pupil:** How many full stops in a bottle of ink?

**Teacher:** Can you tell me how iron was discovered?

**Pupil:** Yes, Miss – they smelt it.

**Teacher:** I have grey wrinkly skin, a long trunk – what am I?

**Pupil:** A liar.

**Teacher:** The law of gravity keeps people on the Earth.

**Pupil:** How did people stay on the Earth before the law was passed?

**Mother:** Why is your nickname toenails?

**Son:** Because I'm at the foot of the class.

**Teacher:** How dare you walk into my class half an hour late.

**Pupil:** OK, I'll come by bike tomorrow.

**Teacher:** Have you learnt anything today?

**Pupil:** No – I've been listening to you.

**Dinner lady:** Eat your greens – they are good for growing children.

**Pupil:** Who wants to grow children?

Did you hear about the music teacher?

He wouldn't accept sick notes.

Teacher: Alexander Graham Bell invented the telephone...

Pupil: That's daft, Miss – who could he phone?

Teacher: Where's your essay on the human brain?

Pupil: It must have slipped my mind, Sir.

Did you hear about the inflatable teacher?

His pupils were always letting him down.

Did you hear about the school trip to Venice?

They came back because it was flooded.

Did you hear about the drama teacher?

She always puts on an act.

Why can't you trust a Maths teacher?

His loyalties are divided.

Jenny: Sir, Mickey keeps pulling my ponytail!

Teacher: I've told you not to bring that horse to school.

How do you make a teacher laugh on a Monday morning?

Tell him a joke on a Friday afternoon.

Teacher: You could get work in the building industry.

Pupil: What as?

Teacher: Two short planks.

Did you hear about the boy who threw a tomato in class?

He was caught red-handed.

Teacher: I told you to write a thousand lines on this paper.

Pupil: I didn't bother – there are enough lines on it already.

**Teacher:** What was James II's first act when he came to the throne?

**Pupil:** Sitting down.

**Teacher:** What did dinosaurs have that no other creature had?

**Pupil:** Baby dinosaurs.

Did you hear about the caretaker who complained that he had nothing to put rubbish in?

He was given the sack.

Did you hear about the boy who took a drum to school?

The teachers told him to beat it.

Teacher: What does minimum mean?

Pupil: A very small mummy.

Teacher: When I was your age I could do problems twice as hard as that.

Pupil: Perhaps you had a better teacher.

Did you hear about the thief who stole prunes from the school kitchen?

He's still on the run.

Teacher: Do you like Beethoven's works?

Pupil: I don't know – what does he make?

Did you hear about the boy who buried his calculator?

Someone told him his batteries were dead.

Teacher: Can anyone tell me something that shrinks when it is washed?

Pupil: Soap.

Teacher: What is the centre of gravity?

Pupil: The letter V, Sir.

Teacher: Why are you late? Didn't your alarm clock go off?

Pupil: It went off alright – but I was still asleep.

What scares teachers?

The school in-spectre.

Teacher: I'm not happy with your daughter's exam results.

Father: Stop giving her exams and cheer yourself up.

Did you hear about the pupil who only washed once a year?

He's in a class of his own.

Did you hear about the pupil who took her history book into the shower?

She wanted to wash behind her years.

Why did the Home Economics teacher cross the road?

It was an idea she cooked up.

Teacher: What is it called when they remove a growth from your head?

Pupil: A haircut.

Why did the Science teacher cross the road?

It was an experiment.

Teacher: How many sexes are there?

Pupil: Three – the male sex, the female sex and insects.

Why did the PE teacher cross the road?

For the exercise.

Teacher: I shall be writing to your father about your poor essay.

Pupil: I don't care – he wrote it.

Teacher: Take your cap off in school.

Pupil: It's not my cap – it's my brother's.

Why did the Geography teacher cross the road?

He was holding his map upside down.

**Teacher:** What is a volcano?

**Pupil:** A sick mountain.

**Teacher:** If I subtract 29 from 87, what's the difference?

**Pupil:** That's what I say – who cares?

**PE teacher:** What do you find the hardest thing about the high jump?

**Pupil:** The ground.

**Pupil:** My pen's run out.

**Teacher:** Well, don't just stand there – go after it.

**Why did the Careers teacher cross the road?**

**He wanted a new direction in life.**

**Why did the Maths teacher cross the road?**

**Search me – it doesn't add up.**

**Teacher: What do we get out of the ground apart from coal and iron?**

**Pupil: Worms.**

**Teacher: How is sawdust produced?**

**Pupil: I dunno.**

**Teacher: Come on – use your head.**

**Why did the English teacher stand in the middle of the road?**

He wanted to read between the lines.

**Teacher: Why can't you repeat what you learnt in history?**

Pupil: I thought history repeated itself.

**Why did the chicken go to school?**

To get an egg-ducation.

**Why did the headmaster cross the road?**

Because he can do anything he likes.

Teacher: What's that bump on your head?

Pupil: That's where a thought struck me.

Teacher: What can a sparrow do that I can't?

Pupil: Wash itself in a saucer.

Why did the Maths teacher throw all the desks out of the classroom?

To make room for the times tables.

Teacher: Name five things that contain milk.

Pupil: Butter, cheese, cream and two cows.

**Pupil:** Why have you given me a plate of maggots?

**Dinner lady:** You asked for the fish dinner.

**Teacher:** Where's your essay on archaeology?

**Pupil:** I didn't want to dig that up again.

Which pirate always gets poor exam results?

Wrong John Silver.

**Teacher:** Where's your essay on the Great Fire of London?

**Pupil:** I couldn't find anything to spark it off.

**Pupil:** Do you serve prawns?

**Dinner lady:** We serve anyone – sit down.

What's the difference between a school dinner and a bucket of pig swill?

The bucket.

**Teacher:** Where did your mother's mother learn her ABCs?

**Pupil:** At gramma school.

What do farmers learn at school?

How to tell ripe from wrong.

Where do whistles
go to school?

In insti-toots.

Why do
thermometers
go to school?

To earn
their degrees.

What did the joker
Maths teacher do?

He played
arithmetricks.

Teacher: Can anyone give
me an example of an
animal that's extinct?

Pupil: A dead skunk, Miss.

**Teacher: What is a fjord?**

**Pupil: It's a car made in Norway, Sir.**

**Teacher: What is an auctioneer?**

**Pupil: It's a man who looks forbidding.**

**Teacher: What is an elderberry?**

**Pupil: It's the oldest type of fruit, Sir.**

**Teacher: What is the collective noun for a group of camels?**

**Pupil: A camelot, Miss.**

Why was the monster good at school?

Because two heads are better than one.

PE teacher: What were you before you came to school?

Pupil 1: Babies, Sir?

Pupil 2: Happy!

Teacher: What is an inkling?

Pupil: It's a very small pen, Sir.

Teacher: That's an excellent essay for someone your age.

Pupil: How about for someone my mum's age?

Teacher: How old are you?

Pupil: I'm not old. I'm nearly new.

Did you hear about the outbreak of laryngitis at school?

Everyone was sent to the croakroom.

PE teacher: Come on – you can run faster than that!

Susie: Sorry, Miss – I'm wearing run-resistant tights.

Teacher: What happened when the wheel was invented?

Pupil: It caused a revolution.

Why are American children healthy?

Because they have a good constitution.

Teacher: How did the Vikings send secret messages?

Pupil: They used Norse code.

Teacher: What does 'moi aussi' mean?

Pupil: I am an Australian.

Pupil: There's a button in my potato.

Dinner lady: It probably came from the jacket.

Music teacher:
It's time for
your violin lesson.

Pupil: Oh, fiddle.

Mother: My daughter
learnt to play the
piano in no time.

Music teacher: Yes,
I've heard her play
like that.

Teacher: Why do
bees hum?

Pupil: Because they
don't know the
words.

Why are rabbits
good at maths?

Because they
multiply well.

Teacher: Why don't we take exams in the jungle?

Pupil: Because of all the cheetahs.

Teacher: Which dinosaur wrote Jane Eyre?

Pupil: Charlotte Brontesaurus.

Teacher: How do dinosaurs pass exams?

Pupil: With extinction.

Teacher: Who went to America on a bicycle?

Pupil: Sir Walter Raleigh.

Teacher: Which adventurer liked mints?

Pupil: Marco Polo.

Teacher: Why mustn't you run in the corridor?

Pupil: Because you might knock someone off their skateboard.

Teacher: School uniform must be worn at all times.

Pupil: Even in the bath, Sir?

Teacher: What was the Cold War?

Pupil: A big snowball fight, Sir.

**Teacher: Do you know the 20th President of the United States?**

**Pupil: No, we were never introduced.**

**Teacher: Did the native Americans hunt bear?**

**Pupil: Not in the winter.**

**Teacher: Where do Finns come from?**

**Pupil: Fish, Miss.**

**Pupil: This soup tastes funny.**

**Dinner lady: Then why aren't you laughing?**

Pupil: Do you have frogs' legs?

Dinner lady: No, I've always walked like this.

Pupil: What's this fly doing in my soup?

Dinner lady: It looks like it's learning to swim.

Pupil: There's a small slug in this lettuce.

Dinner lady: Would you like me to get you a bigger one?

Pupil: There's a caterpillar on my salad.

Dinner lady: It's a good source of protein.

Pupil: There's a fly in my custard.

Dinner lady: I'll fetch him a spoon.

Pupil: There's a fly in my soup.

Dinner lady: Don't worry, that spider on your bread will soon get him.

Pupil: There's a flea in my soup.

Dinner lady: Well tell him to hop it.

Teacher: This coffee is terrible – it tastes like earth.

Other teacher: Mmm – it was ground yesterday.

**Pupil:** There's a fly in my soup.

**Dinner lady:** Just wait until you see the pudding!

**Pupil:** There's a slug in my salad.

**Dinner lady:** Sorry, I'll get you the vegetarian version.

**Pupil:** There is a wasp in my pudding.

**Dinner lady:** So that's where they go in winter.

**Pupil:** There's a cockroach on my plate.

**Dinner lady:** They don't seem to care what they eat do they?

Pupil: There's a maggot in my soup.

Dinner lady: Don't worry, he won't last long in there.

Pupil: There is a spider drowning in my soup.

Dinner lady: It hardly looks deep enough to drown in.

Pupil: There's a mouse in my salad.

Dinner lady: What have you been told about bringing pets to school?

Pupil: There is a worm on my plate.

Dinner lady: That's not a worm – it's your sausage.

**Pupil:** My lunch is talking to me.

**Dinner lady:** That's right – it's a tongue sandwich.

**Pupil:** There's a fly in my soup.

**Dinner lady:** Yes, it's the rotting meat that attracts them.

**Pupil:** There is a beetle in my soup.

**Dinner lady:** Sorry, we're out of flies today.

**Pupil:** What's this spider doing in my alphabet soup?

**Dinner lady:** Probably trying to read.

Pupil: There is a mosquito in my soup.

Dinner lady: Don't worry – they don't eat much.

Pupil: There's a dead fly in my soup.

Dinner lady: It's the heat that kills them.

Pupil: There is a fly in the butter.

Dinner lady: It must be a butterfly.

Pupil: There is a fly in my soup.

Dinner lady: Don't worry I'll call the animal sanctuary.

**Pupil:** There is a fly in my soup.

**Dinner lady:** Hold on, I'll get the fly spray.

**Pupil:** There is a bee in my alphabet soup.

**Dinner lady:** Yes, and I'm sure there is an A, C and all the other letters too.

**Pupil:** There are two flies in my soup.

**Dinner lady:** That's alright – have the extra one on me.

**Pupil:** There is a dead fly in my soup.

**Dinner lady:** Oh no, who will look after his family?

Pupil: What's this cockroach doing on my ice cream?

Dinner lady: Skiing.

Pupil: There is a fly in my soup.

Dinner lady: Don't worry, go ahead and eat it, there are plenty more.

Pupil: There is a dead fly swimming in my soup.

Dinner lady: Don't be silly, dead flies can't swim.

Pupil: There is a fly in my bean soup.

Dinner lady: Don't worry, I'll fish it out and exchange it for a bean.

Pupil: There's a slug in my salad.

Dinner lady: Shhh, or everyone will want one!

Pupil: What is this bug doing in my salad?

Dinner lady: Trying to find its way out.

Pupil: What is this creepy-crawly doing in my salad?

Dinner lady: Not him again!

Pupil: There is a dead fly in my soup.

Dinner lady: No it's not, it's a piece of dirt that looks like one.

**Teacher: What is an astronomer?**

**Pupil: A night watchman, Sir.**

**Dinner lady: You haven't touched your custard.**

**Pupil: I'm just waiting for the fly to stop using it as a trampoline.**

**Teacher: What's an autobiography?**

**Pupil: It's a car's life story.**

**Teacher: What is an astronaut?**

**Pupil: It's a spaceman who scores nothing in his Maths exam.**

**Teacher: What does Brazil produce that no other country produces?**

**Pupil: Brazilians.**

**Teacher: What did Napoleon become after his 39th year?**

**Pupil: 40, Miss?**

**Teacher: Where were the first French fries made?**

**Pupil: In Greece.**

**Why did the teacher give the zombie bad marks?**

**Because he kept making a ghoul of himself.**

**Why is an optician like a teacher?**

**Because they both test pupils.**

**What did the teacher say to the ghost?**

**Don't spook until you're spooken to.**

**Teacher: What happened when Abel died?**

**He became unabel.**

**Teacher: Why is it so wet in Great Britain?**

**Pupil: Because of all the kings and queens that reigned there.**

**Teacher:** What happens to a tree after it's chopped down?

**Pupil:** It's chopped up.

**Teacher:** Which was the highest mountain before Mount Everest was discovered?

**Pupil:** Mount Everest.

**Teacher:** How do you get straight As?

**Pupil:** With a ruler.

**Teacher:** How do you find health, wealth and happiness?

**Pupil:** You open a dictionary, Sir.

Teacher: How many letters are there in the alphabet?

Pupil: Eleven. T-H-E A-L-P-H-A-B-E-T.

Teacher: What did Columbus see on his right hand when he discovered America?

Pupil: Five fingers.

Teacher: How many feet are in a yard?

Pupil: It depends how many people are standing in it.

Music teacher: Why doesn't the piano work?

Pupil: Because it only knows how to play.

Why was the Drama teacher held up by Dick Turpin?

Because he was a stage coach.

Why did the teacher marry the caretaker?

Because he swept her off her feet.

Teacher: What was Noah's profession?

Pupil: He was an arkitect.

Why was the Music teacher arrested?

Because he got into treble.

What diploma do criminals get?

The third degree.

What happened when the school librarian was arrested?

They threw the book at him.

Why is a dictionary dangerous?

Because it has 'dynamite' in it.

Teacher: Who invented the telephone?

Pupil: The Phoenicians?

What does a dog get when it leaves college?

A ped-degree.

Why did the girl who was late for school sit on her watch?

She wanted to be on time.

Which school is it good to drop out of?

Parachute school.

Teacher: What is the difference between the North Pole and the South Pole?

Pupil: The rest of the world.

Teacher: Which nationality is Santa Claus?

Pupil: North Polish.

Why was the boy sent to boarding school?

So that his parents didn't have to help with his homework.

Why couldn't the boy play soccer?

He'd forgotten his socks.

Did you hear about the archery school?

All the pupils had bow legs.

Music teacher: Which composer could never be found?

Pupil: Haydn.

Pupil 1: Do you pray before school dinners at your school?

Pupil 2: No, but we're given the last rites afterwards.

Teacher: I would send your boy to boarding school.

Parent: Why do you say that?

Teacher: Because he's always bored.

Teacher: What does pi have to do with circles?

Pupil: My mum's pies are always round.

Exam question:
Where is talc from?

Answer: Talc is found
on rocks and on
babies.

Exam question: Explain
what a rainbow is.

Answer: Rainbows are
just to look at, not to
really understand.

Exam question:
What is lime?

Answer: Lime is
a rock that
tastes green.

Exam question: What is
fossilization?

Answer: Many dead animals
in the past changed to
fossils, while others
preferred to be oil.

**Exam question: What is genetics?**

**Answer: Genetics explains why you look like your father and if you don't, why you should.**

**Exam question: What is water made up of?**

**Answer: In water, there are twice as many Hs as Os.**

**Exam question: What is E.T. short for?**

**Answer: He's got little legs.**

**Exam question: Explain how winds are formed?**

**Answer: The wind is like the air, only pushier.**

**Exam question: What are clouds?**

**Answer: Clouds are high-flying fogs.**

**Exam question: What is humidity?**

**Answer: Humidity is what you find when you look for air and find water.**

**Exam question: Why is humidity measured?**

**Answer: Humidity is measured so that we won't drown when we breathe.**

**Exam question: What is a cloud bank?**

**Answer: A cloud bank is a place where rain is saved up.**

**Exam question:** If f means forte, what does ff mean?

**Answer:** Eighty.

**Exam question:** What evidence is there of ancient fish?

**Answer:** Fossilized footprints of fishes have been found in rocks.

**Exam question:** What is a blizzard?

**Answer:** A blizzard is when it snows sideways.

**Exam question:** What is a hurricane?

**Answer:** A hurricane is when a breeze gets too big for its boots.

**Exam question: What is a monsoon?**

**Answer: A monsoon is a French gentleman.**

**Exam question: What is thunder?**

**Answer: Thunder is a rich source of loudness.**

**Exam question: What is the fruit of the oak tree called?**

**Answer: A hazel nut.**

**Exam question: Which is the nearest French port to Dover?**

**Answer: Calais – unless you go by aeroplane.**

Exam question: What is unique about maritime law?

Answer: It's very pacific.

Exam question: What did Alexander Graham Bell invent?

Answer: The bell.

Exam question: If a single ticket costs £26.48, how much is a return ticket?

Answer: Twice as much as that.

Exam question: Why are satellites so useful in the communications world?

Answer: Because they're not very heavy.

Exam question: What is economics the study of?

Answer: Economic things.

Exam question: If it is eight o'clock in London, what time is it in Hong Kong?

Answer: More than that.

Exam question: What is artificial respiration commonly known as?

Answer: The kiss of death.

Exam question: Name two of the most important inventions of the 17th century.

Answer: The wheel and false legs.

Exam question: Who was William Wordsworth?

Answer: A poet who felt the call of nature.

Exam question: What is most important in a letter applying for a job?

Answer: You must spell all the words write.

Exam question: What is the currency used in Copenhagen?

Answer: The Denmark.

Exam question: What do the letters HRH stand for?

Answer: Duke of Edinburgh.

**Exam question: Who is the patron saint of travellers?**

**Answer: St Pancras.**

**Exam question: Complete the following: a bird in the hand is worth two...**

**Answer: ...in the pet shop.**

**Exam question: Where did the ancient pharaohs live?**

**Answer: With their mummies.**

**Exam question: What is Charles Darwin best known for?**

**Answer: His book, The Origin of Speeches.**

Exam question: What is the correct name for my father's father?

Answer: George.

Exam question: When did the Signs of the Zodiac first gain popularity?

Answer: In the newspaper.

Exam question: People who suffer from insomnia are called?

Answer: Insomniaphobiacs.

Exam question: How would you share 20p between four men?

Answer: I wouldn't, because it's hardly worth it.

**Exam question: What does migration mean?**

**Answer:** It's a headache that birds get when they fly south for the winter.

**Exam question: How are the 26 letters of the alphabet made up?**

**Answer:** There are five vowels and 30 constants.

**Exam question: Anthropology is the study of what?**

**Answer:** Ants.

**Exam question: Complete the following: A rolling stone gathers...**

**Answer:** ...a fair bit of speed.

Exam question: Who was the leader of the Gunpowder Plot?

Answer: Guy Forks.

Exam question: For what was Stradivarius famous?

Answer: For discovering the upper layer of the atmosphere.

Exam question: Why is one of Handel's best-known works called Water Music?

Answer: Because he lived on an island.

Exam question: If the letters MW appear on a radio, what does it mean?

Answer: Don't play it on top of the microwave.

Teacher: What is a sage?

Pupil: A man who knows his onions.

Exam question: Please say, in no more than 50 words, what you want to do when you leave school.

Answer: I don't know.

Exam question: If Asia is a continent, what is India?

Answer: An island in the Indian Ocean.

Exam question: What is the correct name for the method of providing water for crops in dry areas?

Answer: Irritation.

**Exam question: What is the function of antibodies?**

**Answer: Antibodies are organisations in dispute with people.**

**Exam question: What is the major advantage of passing all your exams?**

**Answer: If you pass all your exams, you're certified.**

**Teacher: What is a monologue?**

**Pupil: An unmarried piece of wood.**

**Music teacher: What is a kettle drum used for?**

**Pupil: It's where the orchestra makes tea.**

Teacher: Give me an example of a paradox.

Pupil: Two doctors, Sir.

Teacher: Give me an example of a quadruped.

Pupil: A four-wheeled moped.

Teacher: What is quicksilver?

Pupil: It's money that gets spent quickly.

Teacher: What is a synonym?

Pupil: It's a word that you use in place of one you can't spell.

**Teacher: What is a siesta?**

**Pupil: It's a car that sleeps in the afternoon.**

**Teacher: What is a tyrant?**

**Pupil: Someone who gets into a temper when he can't tie his tie properly.**

**Teacher: What is a vulgar fraction?**

**Pupil: A fraction with bad manners.**

**Teacher: Give me a sentence with the word 'denial' in it.**

**Pupil: Egypt's main river is denial.**

Teacher: What is the meaning of 'melancholy'?

Pupil: It's a dog that likes melons.

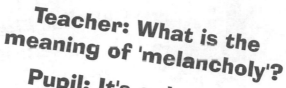

Teacher: Is this the first parent's evening that you've attended?

Parent: No, I once went to one with my mother.

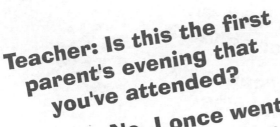

Teacher: What is a climate?

Pupil: It's what you do with a ladder.

Pupil 1: Which fairytale writers were always smiling?

Pupil 2: The Brothers Grin.

**Pupil 1:** Which novelist liked to play Subbuteo?

**Pupil 2:** Charles Flickens.

**Mother:** Do you think Jimmy should have an encyclopedia for school?

**Father:** No, he can walk like everyone else.

**Pupil 1:** Would you say the pupils at your school are tough?

**Pupil 2:** Tough? Even the teachers play truant.

Doctor, doctor, I keep thinking I'm a dog.

How long have you felt this way?

Ever since I was a puppy.

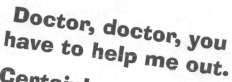

Doctor, doctor, you have to help me out.

Certainly, which way did you come in?

Doctor, doctor, everyone ignores me.

Next!

(Receptionist) Doctor, doctor, the Invisible Man is in reception.

Tell him I can't see him right now.

Doctor, doctor, I keep thinking I'm a pair of curtains.

Pull yourself together, man.

Doctor, doctor, I feel like a doorbell.

Take two pills and give me a ring.

Doctor, doctor, I keep thinking that I'm shrinking.

Now, settle down. You'll just have to be a little patient.

Doctor, doctor, I have a rash that looks like a bowl of strawberries.

I'm sure I have some cream for that.

Doctor, doctor, I broke my leg in two places.

Stay out of those places.

Doctor, doctor, sometimes I think I'm a wigwam and sometimes I think I'm a teepee.

I know your problem — you're two tents.

Why did the monster eat a light bulb?

He wanted a light snack.

Doctor, doctor, I feel like a sheep.

Oh dear, that's baaaaaaaaaad!

Doctor, doctor, I keep thinking I'm a cowboy.

How long have you felt like that?

About a yeeeehaaah!

184

Doctor, doctor, I tend to flush a lot.

Don't worry, it's just a chain reaction.

Doctor, doctor, I keep thinking I'm a bee.

Buzz off!

Doctor, doctor, the pills you gave me for my smelly armpits don't work.

What's wrong with them?

They keep slipping out from under my arms.

Doctor, doctor, my husband smells like fish.

Poor sole.

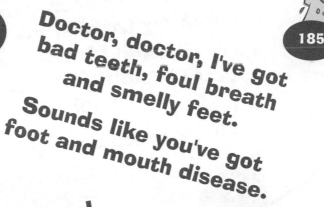

Doctor, doctor, I've got bad teeth, foul breath and smelly feet.

Sounds like you've got foot and mouth disease.

Doctor, doctor, I keep thinking I'm a caterpillar.

Don't worry, you'll soon change!

Doctor, doctor, I'm a burglar.

Have you taken anything for it?

Doctor, doctor, I keep thinking I'm a spider.

What a web of lies.

Doctor, doctor, you've taken out my tonsils, my adenoids, my gall bladder, and my appendix, but I still don't feel well.

That's quite enough out of you.

Doctor, doctor, my baby is the image of his father.

Never mind — just so long as he's healthy.

Doctor, doctor, I feel like a dog.

Sit!

Doctor, doctor, I've lost my memory.

When did this happen?

When did what happen?

Doctor, doctor, I think I'm a rubber band.

Why don't you stretch yourself out on the couch and tell me all about it?

Doctor, doctor, everyone thinks I'm a liar.

I don't believe you.

Doctor, doctor, I think I'm an electric eel.

That's shocking.

Doctor, doctor, I need something to keep my falling hair in.

What about a bag?

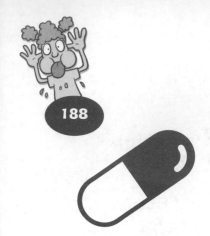

Doctor, doctor, I keep seeing double.

Please sit on the couch.

Which one?

Doctor, doctor, I keep seeing an insect everywhere.

Don't worry — it's just a bug that's going around.

Doctor, doctor, I think I'm a moth.

Get out of the way, you're in my light.

Doctor, doctor, I feel like a needle.

I see your point.

Doctor, doctor,
I have amnesia.

Well, take these pills
— you'll soon forget
about it.

Doctor, doctor, I'm having
trouble with my breathing.

I'll give you something
that will soon put
a stop to that.

Doctor, doctor, what
did the X-ray of my
head show?

Absolutely nothing.

Doctor, doctor, I'm
really ugly! What can I
do about it?

Hire yourself out for
Halloween parties.

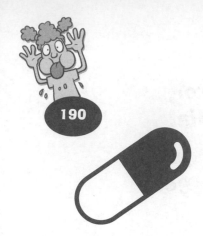

Doctor, doctor, I keep painting myself gold.

Don't worry — it's just a gilt complex.

Doctor, doctor, I can't get to sleep.

Sit on the edge of the bed and you'll soon drop off.

Doctor, doctor, I think I'm a python.

You can't get round me like that, you know.

Doctor, doctor, I feel as sick as a parrot.

Who's a pretty boy then?

Doctor, doctor,
I think I'm a bridge.

What's come over you?

Two cars, a large
truck and a coach.

Doctor, doctor,
I think I'm a moth.

So why did you come here then?

Well, I saw this light at the
window...

Doctor, doctor, I keep
getting pains in the eye
when I drink coffee.

Have you tried taking
the spoon out?

Doctor, doctor, I feel like
a spoon.

Well sit still and don't stir!

Doctor, doctor, have you got something for a bad headache?

Of course, take this hammer and hit yourself on the head. Then you'll have a bad headache.

Doctor, doctor, I feel like a pack of cards.

I'll deal with you later.

Doctor, doctor, I keep thinking there are two of me.

One at a time please!

Doctor, doctor, will this ointment clear up my spots?

I never make rash promises.

Doctor, doctor, I feel like a racehorse.

Take one of these every four laps.

Doctor, doctor, my sister here thinks she's invisible.

What sister?

Doctor, doctor, I feel like a plumber.

You do look a little drained.

Doctor, doctor, I'm boiling up.

Just simmer down.

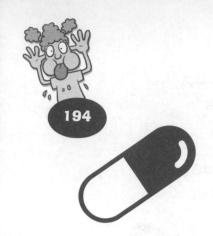

194

Doctor, doctor, can I have a second opinion?

Of course, come back tomorrow!

Doctor, doctor, I keep thinking I'm God.

When did this start?

Well first I created the Sun, then the Earth...

Doctor, doctor, I keep thinking I'm invisible.

Who said that?

Doctor, doctor, I keep thinking I'm a vampire.

Necks please.

Doctor, doctor,
I keep thinking I'm a snake
about to shed its skin.

Go behind the screen and
slip into something more
comfortable.

Doctor, doctor, I feel
like an apple.

We must get to the
core of this.

Doctor, doctor, I think
I'm a yo-yo.

Are you stringing me along?

Doctor: You need new glasses.

Patient: How do you know? I
haven't told you what's wrong with
me yet.

Doctor: I could tell as soon as you
walked in through the window.

Doctor, doctor, I think I'm a snail.

Don't worry — we'll soon have you out of your shell.

Doctor, doctor, I keep thinking I'm a nit.

Will you get out of my hair?

Doctor, doctor, I think I'm a butterfly.

Will you say what you mean and stop flying about?

Doctor, doctor, I think I'm an adder.

Great. Can you help me with my accounts then please?

Doctor, doctor, I think I'm turning into a frog.

You're just playing too much croquet.

Doctor, doctor, I dream there are monsters under my bed. What can I do?

Saw the legs off your bed.

Doctor, doctor, I feel like a packet of biscuits.

Oh, you're crackers.

Doctor, doctor, I'm becoming invisible.

Yes, I can see you're not all there.

Doctor, doctor, my little boy has just swallowed a roll of film.

Let's hope nothing develops.

Doctor, doctor, I snore so loudly I keep myself awake.

Sleep in another room then.

Doctor, doctor, I've a split personality.

Well, you'd better both sit down then.

Doctor, doctor, my son has swallowed my pen, what should I do?

Use a pencil until I get there.

Doctor, doctor, I think I need glasses.

You certainly do, Sir. This is a fish and chip shop.

Doctor, doctor, I keep thinking I'm a dog.

Sit on the couch and we will talk about it.

But I'm not allowed up on the couch!

Doctor, doctor, I've got wind. Can you give me something?

Yes – here's a kite.

Doctor, doctor, how do I stop my nose from running?

Stick your foot out and trip it up.

Doctor, doctor, my baby's swallowed a bullet.

Well don't point him at anyone until I get there.

Doctor, doctor, I've just swallowed a pen.

Well sit down and write your name!

Doctor, doctor, I keep thinking I'm a frog.

What's wrong with that?

I think I'm going to croak.

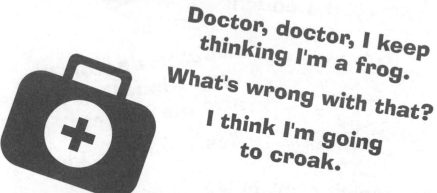

Doctor, doctor, am I a mosquito?

That's your problem, sucker.

Doctor, doctor, how can I cure my sleep walking?

Sprinkle drawing pins on your bedroom floor.

Doctor, doctor, people keep throwing me into bins.

Don't talk rubbish.

Doctor, doctor, I keep hearing a ringing sound.

Try answering the phone.

Doctor, doctor, I keep seeing funny spots before my eyes.

Have you seen a doctor before?

No, just funny spots.

202

Doctor, doctor, I feel like a £50 note.

Go to the shops — the change will do you good.

Doctor, doctor, I keep eating dog food.

I'm a doctor, not a vet.

Doctor, doctor, I think I've broken my neck.

Don't worry — keep your chin up.

Doctor, doctor, I keep thinking I'm a drill.

How boring for you.

Doctor, doctor,
I feel like an untidy nun.
Well, that's a dirty habit.

Doctor, doctor, I feel
like a chair thief.

Please take a seat, then.

Doctor, doctor, can you
recommend anything for
flat feet?

How about a foot pump?

Doctor, doctor, I
think I'm a canary.

Don't worry — it's
tweetable.

204

Doctor, doctor, I keep eating little bits of metal.

That sounds like a staple diet.

Doctor, doctor, I feel like a car.

Park yourself over there a moment.

Doctor, doctor, what's the best cure for dandruff?

Baldness.

Doctor, doctor, I feel like a toilet.

You do look a little flushed.

**What did the surgeon say when he severed an artery?**

**Aorta know better.**

**Doctor, doctor, a dog has just bitten my leg.**

**Did you put anything on it?**

**No, he liked it just the way it was.**

**Doctor, doctor, I think I'm a goat.**

**How long have you thought this?**

**Since I was a kid.**

**Doctor, doctor, I feel like a window.**

**Do you have a pane?**

Doctor, doctor, I just swallowed a worm.

Let me give you something for it.

No thanks — I'll just let it starve.

Dentist: Have your teeth ever been checked?

Patient: No, they've always been white.

Why did the biscuit go to the doctor?

Because it was feeling crummy.

Doctor, doctor, I'm worried about my figure.

You'll just have to diet.

What colour?

Doctor, doctor, I've only got 59 seconds to live!

Just a minute please.

How does an apple a day keep the doctor away?

You have to aim it correctly.

Why is a cold germ stronger than a man?

Because it can bring a man to his sneeze.

Why did the orange go to the doctor?

It wasn't peeling very well.

**208**

Patient: What should I do about my broken leg?

Doctor: Limp.

Doctor, doctor, I feel like a dumpling.

Don't get yourself in a stew.

Doctor, doctor, there's something wrong with my stomach.

Zip up your coat and no one will notice.

Which famous painter always had a cold?

Vincent Van Cough.

Which bird
sounds
like butter?

A stork.

Which well-known
cartoon character
do moths like a lot?

Micky Moth!

How do you get a
wild duck?

Buy a tame one and
annoy it.

What is the wettest
kind of animal?

A raindeer.

How do you stop an elephant charging?

Take away its credit cards.

What do you call a pig that is a thief?

A ham-burglar.

What is another name for a cow?

A lawn moo-er!

What do you call sheep that live together?

Pen friends.

What do you get from a drunk chicken?

Scotch eggs.

Why did the bull rush?

Because he saw the cow slip!

What do you get if you cross a chicken with a bell?

A bird that has to ring its own neck.

What is the best way to make a bull sweat?

Put him in a tight jumper.

Why did the foal cough?

Because he was a little horse.

Why did the cat frown when she passed the house?

She heard fowl language.

How do you know cats don't worry?

They never cry over spilt milk.

What do you call an elephant that is just three feet high?

Trunkated.

What did the skunk say when the wind changed direction?

"Now, it's all coming back to me."

Why did the cat sleep under the oil tank?

Because he wanted to get up oily!

What do you get if you cross a pig with a skunk?

A pig pong!

Who has the most powerful cat in China?

Chairman Miaow!

Why do crocodiles scratch themselves?

Because no-one else would dare.

Now you see it, now you don't – what are you looking at?

A black cat walking over a zebra crossing.

What's the unluckiest cat to have?

A catastrophe!

How is cat food sold?

Usually purr can!

What are bats' favourite jewels?

Tomb stones.

Why are cats good singers?

Because they are very mewsical.

Why don't brave animals get measles?

Because they have no weak spots.

Did you hear about the cat that ate the sofa and two chairs?

He had a suite tooth.

How do you revive a drowning rodent?

Use mouse-to-mouse resuscitation.

What do you call a tiger that's kind and gentle?

A failure.

What do cat actors say on stage?

"Tabby or not tabby."

Why is a sofa like a roast chicken?

Because they are both full of stuffing.

How do you get a cut-price parrot?

Plant bird seed.

What happened when the cat ate a ball of wool?

She had mittens!

What do you get when you cross a cat with a parrot?

A carrot.

What birds spend all their time on their knees?

Birds of prey.

What do you call a killer lion that swims in the sea?

Claws!

What do you call a lion who has eaten your mother's sister?

An aunt-eater.

What is the fiercest flower in the garden?

The tiger lily.

Which big cat should you never play cards with?

A cheetah.

What do tigers sing at Christmas?

"Jungle bells, jungle bells ...!"

Why was the lion-tamer fined?

He parked on a yellow lion!

What do you call a show full of lions?

The mane event!

How are tigers like sergeants in the army?

They both wear stripes.

220

Why did Beethoven get rid of his chickens?

All they said was "Bach, Bach, Bach!"

What do tigers wear in bed?

Striped PJs.

What did the lion say to his cubs when he taught them to hunt?

"Don't go over the road until you see the zebra crossing!"

What flies around at night and can bite off your head?

A tiger moth.

Why did the lion feel sick after he'd eaten the priest?

Because it's hard to keep a good man down.

What does a lion brush his mane with?

A catacomb.

On which day do lions eat people?

On chewsday!

What do you get if you cross a kangeroo with a tiger?

A stripy jumper.

When is a lion
not a lion?

When he turns into
his cage!

What is the
difference between
a lion and a tiger?

The tiger has the
mane part missing!

Where does
a bee go to
the toilet?

The BP station!

Why is the desert lion
everyone's favourite
at Christmas?

Because he has
sandy claws.

What does the lion say to his friends before they go out hunting for food?

"Let us prey."

What kind of money do penguins use?

Iced lolly!

What's a porcupine's favourite food?

Prickled onions.

Where do you find giant snails?

At the end of giants' fingers!

**What do you do when two snails have a fight?**

**Leave them to slug it out!**

**Why is the snail the strongest animal?**

**Because he carries a house on his back!**

**Why shouldn't you take a bear to the safari park?**

**Because it would rather go out to dinner.**

**What do you get if you cross a teddy with a pig?**

**A teddy boar.**

Where do city pigs live?

In sty-scrapers.

Did you hear about the cow that had hiccups?

It churned its own butter.

Do tortoises have good memories?

Yes, they have turtle recall.

What do you get if you cross a goat with a hedgehog?

A kid that's hard to handle.

What do you call a fly with no wings?

A walk.

What do top cats try to achieve?

Purr-fection.

What did the mother bee say to the baby bee?

"Don't bee naughty, honey, just beehive yourself."

Why were the elephants last to leave Noah's Ark?

Because they had to pack their trunks.

What is a frog's favourite ballet?

Swamp Lake.

What do you get if you cross a toad with a galaxy?

Star Warts.

Why do cows lie down when it rains?

To keep each udder dry.

What do you get if you cross a joker with a chicken?

A comedihen!

What do you call a sick crocodile?

An illigator.

What do you call a cheerful hippo?

A happypotamus.

Who designs rabbit warrens?

A burrow surveyor.

What's a horse's favourite game?

Stable tennis.

Did you
hear about
the cat who bought
some bandages?

He wanted to be
a first-aid kit.

What do you
call a camel with
three humps?

Humphrey.

What do you
call a bull when it is
asleep?

A bulldozer.

Why are snakes
bad dancers?

Because they
have no feet.

**What do cats like on their hot dogs?**

Mouse-tard.

**What would happen if pigs could fly?**

Bacon prices would go sky high!

**What's green and very loud?**

A frog-horn.

**What papers do you give to cows to read?**

Daily moos.

What books
do skunks read?

Best smellers.

What's the definition
of a duck?

A chicken with
snow shoes on.

What do you call a
female spider that
never marries?

A spinster.

Why do storks
stand on one leg?

Because if they
didn't, they would
fall over.

What creatures worry about their weight?

Fish – they never go anywhere without their scales.

What do you call a pig running around with no clothes on?

Streaky bacon.

How do frogs send messages to each other?

They use morse-toad!

Did you hear about the two pythons that fell in love?

They had a crush on each other.

What do you call a cat that brings presents?

Santa Claws.

Did you hear about the leopard that had a shower everyday?

He was spotless.

What do bats sing when it's raining?

"Raindrops keep falling on my feet."

How do you cook toast in the jungle?

Put it under a gorilla!

**234**

What do you get if you cross a shark with a set of keys?

Lock jaw.

What do you get if you cross a panda with a harmonium?

Pandamonium.

What do you get if you cross a shellfish with a nuclear warhead?

A guided mussel.

What kind of cars do elephants drive?

Ones with lots of trunk space.

**What is the definition of a guinea pig?**

A very small pig wearing a fur coat.

**What does a battery hen lay?**

Electric eggs.

**How do you stop a dog from being sick in the back of a car?**

Put it in the front.

**Why are monkeys so noisy?**

They were raised in a zoo!

What is a cow's favourite game at parties?

Moo-sical chairs.

What is a snake's favourite school subject?

Hiss-tory!

Did you hear about the sheep dog trials?

The dogs were found not guilty.

What do you get if you cross an elephant with a fish?

Swimming trunks.

**What do you get if you cross a black bird with an idiot?**

**A raven lunatic.**

**What do you get if you cross a rabbit with shallots?**

**Bunions.**

**What happens when hippos get old?**

**They get hippothermic**

**How does an elephant get down from a tree?**

**He sits on a branch and waits for it to break!**

**238**

What's the best place for cats to go on holiday?

The Canary Islands.

Where do sheep get their hair cut?

At the baa-baa's shop.

On which side does a chicken have the most feathers?

On the outside.

Why didn't the maggots go in pairs onto Noah's Ark?

Because they went in apples.

What's the difference between a fish and a piano?

You can't tuna fish.

Why do cows wear bells?

Because their horns don't work.

How did the fish swim a hundred metres in two seconds?

He fell over a waterfall.

What is a pig's favourite ballet?

Swine Lake.

What do you get if you cross a cow with a duck?

Cream quackers.

What do you get if you cross a sheep with a radiator?

Central bleating.

Why could the elephants not go swimming?

Because they only had one pair of trunks.

Why did the pig go shopping to buy bacon?

To get his own back.

What do you call Polly when she jumps from a plane?

Parrotchutist.

Where do jellyfish keep their savings?

In sand banks.

Why are octopuses kings of the ocean?

Because they are so well armed.

What is cowhide used for?

Holding cows together.

**Why did the zebra become a senior police officer?**

**Because he had more stripes than anyone else.**

**What happened to the frog's car when it broke down?**

**It got toad away.**

**Which fish is musical?**

**A piano tuna.**

**Why were the rabbits eating in the middle of the road?**

**It was a dual cabbage-way.**

Why did the fish cross the sea?

To get to the other tide.

What animals use nutcrackers?

Toothless squirrels.

What do boxer dogs do when the door bell rings?

Go into the corner!

Why did the crab get arrested?

Because he kept getting caught pinching things.

Why did the birds fly south for winter?

Because it's too far to walk.

When is a duck not a duck?

When it's afloat!

What always goes to bed with its shoes on?

A horse.

What's the easiest way to count cows?

With a cowculator.

Where do bees go on holiday?

Stingapore!

Why do leopards never escape from the zoo?

Because they're always spotted.

How many ants are needed to fill an apartment?

Ten-ants.

What's the definition of a snail?

A slug with a hard hat on.

What is a frog's favourite sweet?

A lolli-hop.

Where do sick horses go?

Horsepital.

Why do polar bears have a fur coat?

Because they would look silly in a jumper.

What do you get if you cross a pig with a zebra?

Striped bacon.

Why do lions eat their meat raw?

Because they haven't learnt how to cook.

Which dogs smell of onions?

Hot dogs.

Where do bees keep their money?

In a honey box.

What is a goose's favourite fruit?

Gooseberries.

Who paid for lunch when the duck and dog went out?

The duck because she had the bill.

How do you stop mice from squeaking?

Oil them.

How do you stop moles from digging in your garden?

Hide their shovels.

Why did the ant-elope?

Nobody gnu.

What are spiders' webs good for?

Spiders!

Why did the spider buy a car?

He wanted to take it out for a spin.

Why do spiders enjoy waterskiing?

Because they have webbed feet.

What is a baby bee?

A little humbug!

Who is a bee's favourite painter?

Pablo Beecasso!

What kind of insects live on the moon?

Lunar-ticks.

How do you get rid of termites?

Exterminite them.

What did one stick insect say to another?

"Stick around, mate."

What do you call an insect from outer space?

Bug Rogers.

What do you say to an annoying cockroach?

"Stop bugging me."

What do you call an ant that likes to be alone?

Independ-ant.

What did the bee say to the flower?

"Hello honey!"

What lives in gum trees?

**Stick insects.**

What did one firefly say to another?

**"Got to glow now."**

Which bird is always out of breath?

**A puffin.**

What's white and fluffy and floats?

**A cat-emeringue.**

How do you get milk from a witch's cat?

Steal her saucer.

When is it unlucky to see a black cat?

When you are a mouse.

What's a rat's least favourite record?

What's up, Pussycat.

What is small, furry and smells like bacon?

A ham-ster!

What do you get if you cross a mouse with a packet of soap powder?

Bubble and squeak.

Who rode a dog and was a confederate general during the American Civil War?

Robert E Flea!

What do mice do when they move house?

They have a mouse-warming party.

What is grey and hairy and lives on a man's face?

A mousetache.

What's the hardest thing about milking a mouse?

Getting the bucket underneath it.

What would you get if you crossed a dog with a frog?

A croaker spaniel.

What's the definition of a narrow squeak?

A thin mouse.

What fish tastes best with cream?

Jellyfish.

What eats its victims two by two?

Noah's shark.

What happened when two jellyfish met?

They produced jelly babies.

What do you get if you cross an electric eel and a sponge?

Shock absorbers.

Did you hear about the silly jellyfish?

It set!

What is an octo-pus?

An eight-sided cat.

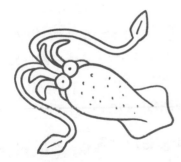

Who held the octopus to ransom?

Squidnappers!

What do you get if you cross a bottle of water with an electric eel?

A bit of a shock!

What's the difference between an African elephant and an Indian elephant?

About 3,000 miles!

Why do elephants cook for themselves?

Because they're the only ones who know what they like to eat!

Elephant Keeper: "My elephant isn't well, do you know a good animal doctor?"

Zoo Keeper: "No, all the doctors I know are people!"

Why are elephants grey?

So you can tell them from flamingos!

How do you tell the difference between an elephant and a mouse?

Try picking them up!

Who writes books for little bees?

Bee-trix potter!

What's the difference between an elephant and a bad pupil?

One rarely bites and the other barely writes!

What's the difference between an injured elephant and bad weather?

One roars with pain and the other pours with rain!

Who's grey, beautiful and wears glass slippers?

Cinderelephant!

What's grey, has a wand, huge wings and gives money to elephants?

The tusk fairy!

What's big and grey with horns?

An elephant marching in a band!

What's grey, carries a bunch of flowers and cheers you up when you're ill?

A get wellephant!

What's grey but turns red?

An embarrassed elephant!

What's grey and lights up?

An electric elephant!

What's as big as an elephant but weighs nothing?

An elephant's shadow!

What's ten feet tall with big teeth and claws?

I don't know, but I'm not sticking around to find out!

What goes up slowly and comes down quickly?

An elephant in a lift!

What's grey and wrinkly and jumps every twenty seconds?

An elephant with hiccups!

What's blue and has big ears?

An elephant at the North Pole!

What weighs four tons and is bright red?

An elephant holding its breath!

What's grey, has four legs and jumps up and down?

An elephant on a trampoline!

Why didn't the dog speak to his foot?

Because it's not polite to talk back to your paw!

What kind of dog sniffs out new flowers?

A bud hound!

What do you call a nutty dog in Australia?

A dingo-ling!

What's more dangerous than being with a fool?

Fooling with a bee!

What's big, grey and flies straight up?

An elecopter!

What's big and grey and has sixteen wheels?

An elephant on roller skates!

What's big and grey and protects you from the rain?

An umbrellaphant!

What's yellow on the outside and grey on the inside?

An elephant disguised as a banana!

Who do fish borrow money from?

A loan shark!

What's blue and highly dangerous?

A shark with a machine gun!

What's small and brown and red?

A sunburnt hamster!

**What's grey
and never
needs ironing?**

**A drip-dry elephant!**

**What's grey with
red spots?**

**An elephant with
the measles!**

**What's grey and goes
round and round?**

**An elephant in a
washing machine!**

**What's grey, stands
in a river when it
rains and doesn't
get wet?**

**An elephant with an
umbrella!**

What's big and grey and wears a mask?

The elephantom of the opera!

What's grey and moves at a hundred miles an hour?

A jet-propelled elephant!

Why does an elephant wear sneakers?

So that he can sneak up on mice!

What time is it when an elephant sits on the fence?

Time to fix the fence!

Why were the elephants thrown out of the swimming pool?

Because they couldn't hold their trunks up!

Why did the elephant paint himself with different colours?

Because he wanted to hide in the colouring box!

How does an elephant get down from a tree?

He sits on a leaf and waits till autumn!

What do you get if you cross an elephant and a kangaroo?

Big holes all over Australia!

Why wasn't the dog hurt when he fell off a 100-foot ladder?

He fell from the bottom rung.

Why was the mother flea so unhappy?

All her children had gone to the dogs.

Why is a toothless dog like a tree?

It has more bark than bite.

Why is a dog so warm in summer?

He wears a coat and pants.

**Why is a dog like a baseball player?**

He runs for home when he sees the catcher coming.

**Why doesn't a dog ever have a nose twelve inches long?**

Because then it would be a foot.

**Why does a dog scratch himself?**

He is the only one that knows where it itches.

**Why do dogs turn around two times before lying down?**

One good turn deserves another.

Why do dogs lie down?

They can't lie up!

What is the definition of a zebra?

A horse behind bars.

What do you call a stupid ape?

A chumpanzee.

Where do pigs go for their holidays?

Nowhere, they sty at home.

What's big and purple and barks a lot?

A grape dane.

How does an elephant climb a tree?

It sits on an acorn and waits for it to grow.

What is the definition of a skunk?

An animal with a phew bad habits.

Why didn't the dog play cards on his ocean cruise?

Because the captain stood on the deck.

Why didn't the boy advertise in the paper when his dog was lost?

His dog never read the paper.

273

Why did the thoughtful father buy his six children a dachshund?

He wanted a dog they could all pet at once.

Why did the police dog not look like a dog?

He was in the secret service.

Why did the dog's owner think his dog was a great mathematician?

When he asked the dog what six minus six was, the dog said nothing.

What type of sandals do frogs wear?

Open-toad.

Why did the dog sleep so poorly?

He plugged his electric blanket into the toaster by mistake, and kept popping out of bed all night!

Why did the dog take a bag of oats to bed at night?

To feed his night-mares.

Why did the cat sleep on the chandelier?

He was a light sleeper.

What's a dolphin's favourite TV show?

Whale of fortune!

What kind of money do fishermen make?

Net profits.

Why did the dog run in circles?

He was a watchdog, and needed winding.

Why did the dog jump up and down on the potato patch?

He hoped to make mashed potatoes.

Why did the dog jump off the Empire State Building?

He wanted to make a hit on Broadway.

Which fish go to heaven when they die?

Angelfish.

Why are camels such poor ballroom dancers?

They have two left feet.

Who gave the dog a black eye?

Nobody gave it to him. He had to fight for it.

Which side of a dog has the most hair?

The outside.

Which dog looks like a cat?

A police dog in disguise.

Which dog is always without a tail?

A hot dog.

Which fish only swims at night?

A starfish.

What do you call a fish with no eyes?

Fsh!

Where was the dog when the lights went out?

In the dark.

Where do you usually find dogs?

It all depends on where you lose them.

When you catch your dog eating a dictionary, what should you do?

Take the words right out of his mouth.

When is a dog most impolite?

When he points.

When do dogs have sixteen legs?

When there are four of them.

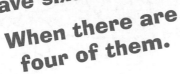

What would you get if you crossed a chicken with a dog?

A hen that lays pooched eggs.

What do you get if you cross an abbot with a trout?

A monkfish!

**Who has eight guns and terrorises the ocean?**

**Billy the squid.**

**What time is it when your watchdog lets a robber take the family silver?**

**Time to get a new watchdog.**

**What time is it when five dogs are chasing a cat down the street?**

**Five after one.**

**What should you know before you teach your dog a new trick?**

**More than your dog!**

What should you do with a blue dog?

Cheer him up.

What should you do if you see a vicious dog?

Hope he doesn't see you.

What place of business helps dogs who have lost their tails?

A retail store.

What should you do if you find a 500-pound dog wearing your favourite tie?

Go see a doctor. You have been seeing too many 500-pound dogs lately.

What should you do if you find an angry 500-pound dog in your kitchen?

Eat out.

What should you do if you find a 500-pound dog asleep on your bed?

Sleep on the sofa.

What looks like a dog, sounds like a dog, eats like a dog, but isn't a dog?

A pup.

What is worse than a dog howling at the moon?

Two dogs howling at the moon.

What do you call a dangerous fish that drinks too much?

A beer-a-cuda!

What do bees do with their honey?

They cell it.

What do you get if you cross a cat with a dog?

An animal that chases itself.

What's a paw-paw?

A puppy's foot-foot.

284

What do you get when you cross a cow with a duck?

Milk quackers.

In what month do dogs bark least?

In February – it's the shortest month.

Why did King Kong climb the Empire State building?

Because he couldn't fit in the lift.

What do you call a pig with three eyes?

A piiig.

What goes 'quick, quick'?

A duck with hiccups.

Why don't bats live alone?

They like to hang around with their friends.

What did the gorilla call his first wife?

His prime-mate!

What do you call a mosquito with a tin suit?

A bite in shining armour.

What's pink and grey and has four feet?

A hippopotamus poking its tongue out.

What do giraffes have that no other animal has?

Baby giraffes.

How do you find a lost gorilla?

Hide in a tree and make a noise like a banana.

Why is a bunny the luckiest animal in the world?

Because it has four rabbits' feet.

Why do elephants never forget?

Because nobody ever tells them anything.

What bird can be heard at meal times?

A swallow.

What is green and squirts something red?

A chameleon eating a hot dog with ketchup!

What's in the middle of a jellyfish?

A jellybutton.

288

Why can't you play jokes on snakes?

Because you can never pull their legs.

How do you stop a snake from striking?

Pay it decent wages!

Where do frogs go to get their eyes tested?

A hoptitions.

What's small, cute and purple?

A kitten holding its breath.

What do you get if you cross a frog and a rabbit?

A rabbit that says ribbit.

What did the parrot say to the spaniel?

"I'm a cocker-too!"

Why do giraffes take so long to apologise?

Because it takes a long time for them to swallow their pride.

Did you hear about the man that took his dog to obedience classes?

The dog passed with flying colours, but he failed!

**What animal would it be nice to be on a cold day?**

**A little otter!**

**Did you hear about the mole that ate three tins of baked beans?**

**He got wind in the willows.**

**Did you hear the joke about the lion?**

**No.**

**When you do, it will make you roar.**

**Did you hear about the girl that found some milk bottles in a field?**

**She thought she'd found a cow's nest!**

Did you hear about the bull that swallowed a bomb?

He was a-bomb-in-a-bull!

Did you hear about the bull called Terry?

He was Terry-bul.

Did you hear about the fight in the fish shop?

All the fish got battered.

What did the lovesick bull say to the cow?

"When I fall in love, it will be for heifer!"

Why did the baby turkey bolt down his food?

Because he was a little gobbler!

How do sheep keep warm in the winter?

Central bleating!

What do you call a pig that took a plane?

Swine flu.

Why do ducks have webbed feet?

To stop them from sinking in the mud!

Why did the rooster refuse to fight?

Because he was a chicken.

What do you get if you feed cows money?

Very rich milk.

Why do dinosaurs walk on two legs?

To give ants a chance.

What do you call a crazy chicken?

A cuckoo-cluck.

What do you get
if you cross a cow,
a sheep and a goat?

The milky bar kid.

What did the
well-mannered sheep
say to his friend at
the shed door?

"After ewe
my friend."

What gives milk,
and makes cows'
dreams come true?

A dairy godmother.

Why couldn't the
elephant travel on
the train?

Because his trunk
wouldn't fit on the
luggage rack.

**How many sheep does it take to make a jumper?**

None, sheep can't knit.

**Why didn't the pig listen to his father?**

Because he was such an old boar.

**What do you get if you put a young goat in a food mixer?**

A mixed-up kid!

**What do you get if you cross a terrier with a vegetable?**

A Jack Brussel.

Why did the idiot put his chicken in a hot bath?

Because he wanted her to lay hard-boiled eggs.

What do you call a cricket in a space ship?

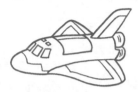

A space hopper.

What did Lady Godiva's horse do when it realised she wasn't wearing any clothes?

It shyed.

What is the difference between a black chicken and a white chicken?

Black chickens can lay white eggs, but white chickens can't lay black eggs.

"Doctor, doctor, I think I'm a puppy!"

"Sit down please."

"I can't, I am not allowed on the sofa!"

What do you get if you cross a cow with a mule?

Milk with a kick in it.

Why did the elephant cross the road?

To pick up the flattened chicken.

What is grey and sniffs?

An elephant with a cold.

What do you give a sick pig?

Oinkment.

What is the difference between a crocodile and a biscuit?

You can't dip a crocodile in your tea.

What do you get if you are allergic to horses?

Bronco-itis.

Mary had a bionic cow,
It lived on safety pins.
And every time she milked that cow,
The milk came out in tins.

"Waiter, waiter, have you got frogs' legs?"

"No Sir, I always walk like this."

What do you get if a sheep walks under a cloud?

A sheep that's under the weather!

What do you get if you cross Bambi with a ghost?

Bamboo!

Why should a school not be near a chicken farm?

To stop the pupils from learning fowl language.

300

"Doctor, doctor my wife thinks she's a duck!"

"You better bring her in to see me straight away."

"I can't do that, she has already flown south for the winter."

What fish do dogs chase?

Catfish.

Why was the mother kangeroo cross with her children?

Because they ate fries in bed.

What is black, has six legs, is heavily disguised and makes people scream?

A computer bug.

How do you spot a cool spider?

He has his own website.

When does a horse have six legs?

When it has a jockey on its back.

If a crocodile makes shoes, what does a banana make?

Slippers.

What pet makes the loudest noise?

A trumpet.

What's the fastest fish in the sea?

A motorpike!

Have you ever seen a dog make a rabbit hutch?

No, but I've seen a fox make a chicken run.

What do you get if you cross a nun and a chicken?

A pecking order.

Why is a turkey like an evil little creature?

Because it is always a-goblin.

**What swings through trees and is very dangerous?**

**A chimpanzee with an axe.**

**Why does an ostrich have such a long neck?**

**Because its head is so far from its body.**

**What's a mermaid?**

**A deep-she fish.**

**Where do cows go for lunch?**

**The calfeteria.**

304

Which animals are the snootiest?

The ones that live in trees – they look down on all the other creatures.

How do you hire a teddy bear?

Put him on stilts!

What did the slug say to the other slug who had hit him and run off?

"I'll get you next slime!"

What was the snail doing on the highway?

About one mile a day!

How do snails get their shells so shiny?

They use snail varnish!

What did the maggot say to his friend when he got stuck in an apple?

"Worm your way out of that one!"

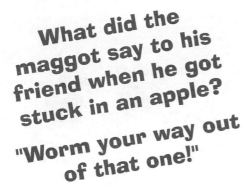

What's black and white and green?

A frog sitting on a newspaper.

What is worse than finding a maggot in your apple?

Finding half a maggot in your apple!

306

Where do sheep get shorn?

At the baa baas!

How can you tell which end of a worm is which?

Tickle it in the middle and see which end laughs!

Why does a rooster watch TV?

For hentertainment!

What do you get if you cross a chicken with a cement mixer?

A brick-layer.

What do you call a farmyard cat?

Puss in boots.

What do you get if you cross a dog with a mole?

You get holes all over your house!

What happens when a dog keeps eating bits off the dresser?

He gets splinters in his mouth.

What do you get if you cross a dog with a skunk?

A very smelly house.

What language do birds speak?

Pigeon English.

What is a snake's favourite dance?

The mamba!

Why is a reindeer like a gossip?

Because they are both tail bearers!

What would happen if bulls could fly?

Beef would go up!

What do you get from an Alaskan cow?

Cold cream!

What do you get if you sit under a cow?

A pat on the head!

How do you stop a rooster crowing on Sunday?

Eat him on Saturday!

Why did the reindeer wear sunglasses at the beach?

Because he didn't want to be recognised!

Why did Bo Peep lose her sheep?

She had a crook with her!

Which bug does amazing motorcycle stunts?

Evil Boll Weevil.

How can you make a tarantula shake?

Run up behind it and say BOO!

Where do you find reindeer?

It depends on where you leave them!

Which bug gobbles up trash?

The litterbug.

What do you get if you cross a hen with a dog?

Pooched eggs!

What do snake charmers wear around their necks?

Boa-ties.

Where do sheep go on holiday?

The Baaahamas!

312

Why did the farmer call his pig 'Ink'?

Because he kept running out of his pen!

How do you stop a dinosaur from biting his nails?

I give up.

Pull his foot out of his mouth.

What kind of maths do owls like?

Owlgebra.

Which is the bossiest ant?

Tyrant!

What kind of bears like to go out in the rain?

Drizzly bears.

"Ask me if I'm a rabbit."

"Okay. Are you a rabbit?"

"Yes, I'm a rabbit. Now ask me if I'm a caribou."

"Okay, are you a caribou?"

"No, silly. I just told you I'm a rabbit."

What do snakes learn in school?

Reading, writhing and arithmetic.

**What do you call a confused bee?**

**A maybee.**

**Why did the rabbit go to the doctor?**

**Because he felt jumpy.**

**What happened to the two bedbugs who fell in love?**

**They were married in the spring.**

**Why can't you tell secrets on a farm?**

**Because the corn has ears, the potatoes have eyes, the grass whispers and the horses carry tails.**

**What did the Cinderella fish wear to the ball?**

**Glass flippers.**

**What did the duck say when it laid a square egg?**

**"Ouch!"**

**When is it socially correct to serve milk in a saucer?**

**When you're feeding the cat.**

**How do you tell the difference between an elephant and a rhinoceros?**

**The elephant has a better memory.**

What does a frog say when it washes car windows?

"Rub it, rub it, rub it."

What do you call it when giraffes moving one way get mixed up with giraffes moving another way?

A giraffic jam.

What has feathers and writes?

A ballpoint hen.

What do moose do at a concert?

Make moosic.

Which bird lives underground?

A mynah bird.

Which ant is an army officer?

Sergeant!

What do monkeys eat for dessert?

Chocolate chimp cookies.

What do you call ants from abroad?

Import-ants.

What is a kangeroo's favourite food?

Hop-suey.

Why did the lobster get arrested?

It pinched a fish.

What happened to the chicken that went sunbathing?

It got fried.

What animal is good at baseball?

A bat.

Did you hear about the angry hare?

It was hopping mad.

Where did the prehistoric cow live?

In a mooseum.

What did the mummy buffalo say to her son when he went away?

"Bison."

How does an elephant hide in a cherry tree?

He paints his toenails red.

What kind of wig can hear?

An earwig.

What do you get if you cross a rat with an owl?

A bird that's ugly but doesn't give a hoot!

What sort of hair do sea lions have?

Wavy.

What's the difference between a cat and an alien?

Lots of stars and space!